Acknowledgment:

In writing my thesis I am indebted to various people from the University of Groningen, especially Professor Johan Woltjer who without his directions and guidance, I would never manage to finish my thesis.

I am also indebted to all who have given time, encouragement, information, contributions and criticism, and particularly great thanks goes to Dr. Ahmad Abu Khater who helped a lot in clearing several issues. Many thanks to all the people who helped me during interviews, thank you all for all the material and insights.

Special thanks goes also to Dr. Katharina Gugerell, for he kind words at the thesis presentation Symposium.

Last but not least, a big thanks goes to my loving and encouragement wife Sondos, whom managed to keep my son quite during my studies, Thank you for everything,

Executive summary

Water situation is Middle East is hard and difficult to make sense out of it; indicators of shortage are hard to examine and argue. Talking about water in Middle East has many dimensions, social, environmental, religious, and political. What can be drawn from all of this is that water in Middle East is a highly sensitive political issue.

Water, poses the biggest challenge of all natural resources, especially when it comes to the Middle East, an area known for its shortage and limited fresh water resources. Water shortage is not the only reason for causing water conflicts, fair equitable agreements plays an essential role in the water conflict especially among states sharing trans-boundary waters.

Water war as a concept may not mesh with the conventional construct of warfare. Water wars can be waged and won by nonmilitary means, such as by reengineering trans-boundary flows. But when military force has been employed by any country to change the regional water map, this research attempt to show that merely water conflicts in Middle East are political issues. Hydro-politics is quickly becoming a subject of crucial importance within the general field of conflict studies and environmental politics

This research is motivated by the Middle East water conflict, which exhibits many aspects of other conflicts over natural resources around the world. Particularly, the Jordanian-Israeli conflict is very intriguing as it incarnates a situation in which conflicting representations of fresh water resources, coupled with power structure imbalance, have created tension, injustice, instability and resulted in a long lasting conflict

The conflict over water facing the nations in the Middle East today will become even more serious over the next coming years, unless something is done in proper time future. Populations are growing and the standard of living is expected to increase as well, Averting water conflicts, demands fair treaties, cooperation, water sharing and not dividing, Joint Fact Finding, Transparency, and clarity are the most essential elements. Despite the ubiquity of transnational basins, the number of genuine water-sharing treaties in the world, unfortunately, remains remarkably small. Most trans-boundary river, in fact, lacks any treaty-based arrangements to promote cooperation between co-riparian states.

Table of Contents

List of Tables:

List of Figures

Chapter One
Trans-boundary water conflict dilemma

1.1. Introduction:

Waters are never the same: some waters are accessible, manageable, cheap, some other waters are more socially valued or even more peaceful, some waters are more contested and violent, or less multi-functional, some waters are conflict free, and some other waters are more limited and more negotiable, some waters are linked with the sovereignty of the states.

Water situation is Middle East is hard and difficult to make sense out of it; indicators of shortage are hard to examine and argue. Talking about water in Middle East has many dimensions, social, environmental, religious, and political. what can be drawn from all of this, is that water in middle east is a highly sensitive political issue.

This research focuses on trans-boundary water conflicts; on the personal level the topic is of a huge interest since 2007 when for the first time realized the importance of the issue by working on mega reviving projects in Jordan valley, on the other hand this topic is highly regarded in Middle East, considering the national level and the critical nature to the geo-politics of the area. The problem is of a multi-level nature, multi-dimensional. On the global level world's water resources are not evenly distributed, and in most cases are not necessarily distributed according to the political boundaries, water conflicts often cross national borders(Trolldalen 1997), parties of "trans-boundary water conflict" may not reach any agreement on proper principles (namely distribution and allocation of existing sources) in the face of an absolute supply rationale. One must work, with the assumption of one single society either Israel or Jordan, the assumption that this society will face a common challenge in the coming future, when its total potential of fresh water is fully exploited for drinking purposes. (Biswas 1994)(Alkhaddar et al. 2005).

By the term trans-boundary Water conflict, we refer to the conflict among two or more sovereign states over the access to control the water resources of an international river basin (trans-boundary) that traverses the territories of many states. As stated by (Trottier & Slack 2004)'Water conflicts will cause the wars of the future.' In my research I'm attempting to deconstruct and reexamine this argument: it is the object of numerous arguments and counter-arguments in the scientific community (Abukhater 2013; Allan 1998; Al-Kharabsheh & Ta'any 2005; Benvenisti 2004; Berman & Wihbey 1999; Biswas 1994; Dabelko 2004; I. Fischhendler 2008a; Fisher 2001; Fisher & Huber-Lee 2011; Franklin M. Fisher 2010; Frederiksen 1999; Jain & Singh 2010; Lowi 2003; Susskind & Shafiqul Islam 2013; Wolf 1996; Zeitoun & Warner 2006a)as much effort has been devoted to either proving or disproving the causal connection between water scarcity and water wars.

The conflict over water facing the nations in the Middle East today will become even more serious over the next coming years, unless something is done in proper time future. Populations are growing and the standard of living is expected to increase as well, resulting in increased demand for domestic and urban water supplies required to meet the essential needs, while the amount of the natural water resources available remains more or less fixed. Water from additional non-conventional sources such as recycling, desalination and import are all possible particularly in an era of peace and cooperation. (Shuval & Dweik 2007)

This work attempts to provide a comprehensive review of the relevant literature on managing water conflicts around the world. Current trends and projections suggest that conflicts based on water scarcity escalate when the issue is not addressed effectively and in a timely manner(Heather L. Beach, Jesse Hammer 2000). Proactive efforts to prevent these conflicts have been overwhelmed by pessimistic forecasting. This situation negatively affects multilateral cooperative efforts and results in attempts to pursue unilateral short-term gains and in some cases increases in military power. So far, few comprehensive and interdisciplinary analyses of such international surface water conflicts have been produced. Only fragmented findings and scattered experimentations endeavors are available to the conflict resolution community.

Consequently, water has been exaggeratedly presented as a source of great conflicts. This, which poses a potential obstacle to a long-term peace agreement, could be seen as a positive thing, however, in the sense that water could propitiously be a source of cooperation, rather than a *casus belli* (Fisher, *et al.*, 2001) In such arid regions.

Water is an extremely precious resource that evidently triggered wars in the past and could possibly be the reason for peace in the future. In support of this argument that water, if not utilized as a vehicle for peace and stability (Abukhater 2013), can potentially be a source of conflict and war, as stated by Kofi Anan at the World Day for Water 2001, and king Hussein "The one issue that could bring Jordan to war again is water." (Bard 2007)

Mirumachi & Nakayama (2007), argues that "there is a growing consensus that water scarcity is not the major and sole factor that prompts war…" rather than the inequality of water allocation is the major cause of *hydro-hostility* (and therefore excavation of water) instead of *hydro-stability* and multi-national cooperation. Priscoli & Wolf

(2008) states, "application of an equitable" water-sharing agreement along the volatile waterways of the world is a prerequisite to hydro-political stability which, finally, could help pushing political forces away from conflict in favor of cooperation." He also adds, "Not surprisingly, up-stream riparian's have advocated that the emphasis between the two principles be on „equitable utilization," since that principle gives the needs of the present the same weight as those of the past. Likewise, down-stream riparian's (along with the environmental and development communities).

A wide spectrum of conflict resolution methods are developed and considered to manage equitable sharing of trans-boundary water resources. Nevertheless, severe conflicts over trans-boundary waters still exist, where a state receives more water than its actual need, and other states perish of no water allocated. Developing and applying equitable principles over trans-boundary water allocation processes tends to foster optimal water management, which procures an atmosphere conducive for seeding cooperation and rooting out altercation, to hold a grip on such concept is essential in shaping a successful water cooperation future for everybody.

1.2. The Importance of the research and the main research questions:

The research intends to draw attention to the urgency and complexity of water conflict issues facing Jordan-Israel. The research will shed light on a number of issues ranging from trans-boundary water conflict, water dispute, negotiation and water diplomacy, in an attempt to examine thoroughly the peace treaty among both countries and reflect over future political agendas, the research will examine the threats, obstacles and opportunities, and the ability to develop a joint water future vision.

Conflict over water is considered as one of the wicked problem, the characteristics of complex wicked problems is that they are highly situational dependent, and each case is considered as a unique case by itself (Hartmann 2012), accordingly the literature indicates that while in many areas there has been extensive research and analysis, there continues to be an urgency for further studies on the specific situations that lead to conflicts over water and other environmental resources(Heather L. Beach, Jesse Hammer 2000).

The Hydro-Politics is quickly becoming a subject of crucial importance within the general field of conflict studies and environmental politics (Sherman 1999)(Williams 2002). Yet the subfield as a whole remains at a cradle stage. Whereas scientists and environmentalists continue to predict the very real likelihood of severe global water scarcity in the next fifty years, the political ameliorations and ramifications on the other hand, both in terms of state sovereignty and supranational stability, and the general linkages between global environmental changes and political and state sovereignty, are not as clearly understood. The purpose of this study is to draw a clearer perspective of the trans-boundary water conflict, and to attempt to a better understanding of the process of conflict resolution mechanism.

This research is motivated by the Middle East water conflict, which exhibits many aspects of other conflicts over natural resources around the world. Particularly, the Jordanian-Israeli conflict is very intriguing as it incarnates a situation in which conflicting representations of fresh water resources, coupled with power structure imbalance, have created tension, injustice, instability and resulted in a long lasting conflict.

1.3. The purpose of the research:

This Research Thesis comes as a fulfillment for obtaining a M.Sc. degree in Environmental and Infrastructure planning, the main focus is trans-boundary water conflict issues, the area of research will be the trans-boundary water issues among the Hashemite kingdom of Jordan and The state of Israel.

Throughout the Middle East, asymmetries of a complex hydro-political network interplays and tries to control water supported by military power. The current allocation arrangements of the region's major river basins, the lake Tiberius, the Jordan river and Yarmouk river are the emergent sources of tension, and potential sources of conflict and violence. Of all the Middle East's river basins, however, it is the Jordan River that hosts the most violent troubled and combustible conflict. (Kubursi 2006).

The literature indicates (Zeitoun & Warner 2006a; Zeitoun 2008; Wolf et al. 2003; Wolf 1996; Susskind & Shafiqul Islam 2013; Wardam 2004; Trottier & Slack 2004; Velma I. Grover 2007; Steenhuis 2010; Shuval 2011)that while in many areas there has been extensive research and analysis, there continues to be a need for more studies on the specific situations that lead to conflicts over water and other environmental resources related to the trans-boundary waters among Israel and Jordan.

2. Chapter Two
Methods and Methodology

2.1. Introduction:

This chapter aims to provide a detailed description of the research methodology, including key questions, hypotheses, and methodological design adopted for conducting this study. Furthermore, this part presents a methodical account of (and justification for) employing detailed case study analysis for a robust methodological design. The research methodology explained in this chapter will be applied in the case selection and analysis parts of the research which will be guided by the logic model developed in this chapter.

This study attempt to research the intricacies of the water conflict, among Jordan and Israel, one of the central questions in the peace process among both states. the main focus will be the international water conflict from a foreign policy decision making point of view between Jordan and Israel, it will attempt to analyze the water conflict between both states, out of the great diversity of conflict knowledge, it is possible to extract some fundamental insights that seem to hold true for the current water conflicts.

The purpose of reflecting on a number of theories is related to the long pace of conflict, the conflict started since the establishment of the state of Israel, focusing on a one theory will bring a reductionist point of view, and will only show a facet of the conflict, to gain a better understanding of the conflict drawing over a number of theories will be of a great help.

To present them in an easily understandable manner, focus on general theories of managing shared water resources between states, presenting these theories in a clear comprehendible way. The research will also explore the capabilities of the following theories and rhetoric's:

- Theory of conflict,
- Water, and power (*hydro-politics*);
- Water wars rhetoric;
- water equity and international law
- Negotiation Theory
- Water Diplomacy

The research is considered to be a qualitative research showing the actual water conflict in literature and socio-scientific way, and the possibility of adapting a new theory of conflict resolution

Traditionally, water has not been the most prominent aspect of Israeli–Arab confrontations. Other issues; such as the question of territorial rights, equitable and secure borders, the plight of refugees; date back further and have provided more newsworthy headlines. However, since the late eighties, the role of water has become largely the backbone of contention between states. many Arab leaders, including those who are considered to be the most moderate, such as late King Hussein of Jordan and former UN Secretary General, Boutrus Boutrus-Ghali, who have warned on several occasions that water is a critical issue, to instigate and become the cause of a future Israeli–Arab war (Sherman 1993; Zeitoun & Warner 2006a; Selby 2005).

2.2. Why the quantitative approach?

The importance of point of view is concisely expressed in a remark often attributed to Isaac Newton: "If I have seen farther, it is by standing on the shoulders of giants" (reported by Catherine Drinker Bowen in Merton, 1985). Well the importance of point of view emerges explicitly in many settings. Under conditions in which subjects are not able to explore and communicate freely, hydro/economo/techno water scarcity differences become disagreements that are difficult to resolve. Techniques of conflict resolution requires a full knowledge of all the variables of the problem from both sides, qualitative research methods are one way of measuring and comparing between the point of view of each state, it could be considered a trustful method of weighting. one of the draw backs of quantitative research related to conflict studies is their dependence on data, the data and numerical research is that official data are mostly given by governmental bodies, these bodies tend to stretch the data and in some cases to exaggerate numbers to fit their own political agendas, it's more a game theory, the other setback that data from non-governmental research bodies tend to have a huge discrepancies between each other, and the discrepancies are highly distrustful, in this case I leave it to the reader to judge.

The outcome of this thesis is a different way of overlooking conflict resolution, since all theories and practices had failed to a certain point of bring peace and resolution a new approach have been proposed by several researchers among Shafiqul, Susskind, AbuKhater, and several others. This thesis will attemp to understand the characteristics of water conflict in the context of the Jordanian-Israeli water conflict.

2.3. Research Questions and hypothesis:

The attempt of my thesis is to construct an argument for transformative approach to water conflict resolution, also water allocation decision must be understood in its unique historical political and hydrological context the thesis will make a careful prescriptive advice mechanism that will be useful for water negotiators.

Many researchers (Susskind & Shafiq Islam 2013; Abukhater 2013) have insisted that The persistence of water conflicts in many arid regions all over the globe lies in the way of considering resources, water has been simply considered as a rare, scarce and limited resource, this conception of water made reaching an equitable water resource allocation an unachievable task, and triggered toward more adverse impacts of hostility and resentment.

To serve the purpose of the research outlined in previously, the research seeks to explicate three key questions:

1. **Q1:** The cardinal question is: **what are the characteristics of the Jordanian Israeli water conflict**? Realists argue that the political-structural condition of anarchy, the absence of a common government, in the international system has an impact on the willingness of states to engage in cooperation (Lowi 2003). Water Conflict may be viewed as occurring along (political), (ecological), and (social) dimensions. This three-dimensional perspective can help us understand the complexities of conflict and why a conflict sometimes seems to proceed in contradictory directions.

2. **Q2: What are the lessons that can be learned** from the theory and practice of the concept of water

allocation equitable concepts in water negotiation in general? This question may be answered by breaking it into a number of sub questions:

a. **SUB-Q2.1**: how negotiation could lay a fertile ground for reconciliation of trans-boundary water conflict issues

b. **SUB-Q2.2** what are the toolkit of the negotiator to reach a common ground among counter parties?

c. **SUB-Q2.3** is the process always predictable or should uncertainty be considered?

To be able answering such a problematic question which are seemingly context-specific, is considered a challenge in itself, it is necessary to formulate concrete, flexible and adaptable, parameters of process enquiry, a set of assumptions layered into the main questions that will be explained and then examined in the research:

- **Hypothesis 1**: Hydro Politics in the forms of (*hydro-hostility, Hydro-hegemony* and *hydro-stability*)are the outcomes of the interstate policies,

- **Hypothesis 2**: the states perception of equity in water allocation is the hidden force that moves its tendencies towards resolution and reconciliation.

- **Hypothesis 3**: The political conflict between riparian states serves as an opportunity to cooperation

- **Hypothesis 4:** Water cooperation is a potential vehicle for future conflict resolution and reconciliation. Cooperation can promotes *hydro-stability,* while competitive approaches may lead *to hydro-hostility*

2.4. Research Methods

The choice of a research strategy depends on the purpose of the study, since that will guide the kind of information one is interested in finding. This research is a case study of a qualitative nature since that method is considered to be the most appropriate when analyzing events or process such as the water conflict resolution and the negotiation mechanism.

The study focuses on how actors and structures have affected the water negotiations and implementation process between Israel and Jordan. Thus it is an analysis that focuses predominantly on process, but also on outcome.

The qualitative case study method is seen as appropriate when an analysis seeks to improve the understanding of the dynamics behind social and political processes in areas where contentious issues are discussed, the strength of single case study data collection is that it permits the researcher to use several different sources in detail, the case study method is often used in empirical studies that involve context-dependent contemporary events. In addition studies that rely on cases are more likely to result in unexpected findings(Platt 1988).

My own reason for choosing the qualitative case study method is related to the acknowledgement that context is imperative to understanding the conflict over trans-boundary water resources. The approach that will be a hybrid deductive and inductive; Hence this approach recognizes the interplay of the terrain between theory and empirical material. By using this approach I have had the privilege and the opportunity to formulate and reformulate theoretical ideas on the basis of my empirical findings. The power of such approach enables researcher to use theoretical tools from other disciplinary backgrounds. However, it is my aim to provide enhanced knowledge and understanding through an analysis of an ongoing process of moving from conflict to cooperation.

2.5. Literature Review and Theoretical Framework

Issues of trans-boundary water conflict have appeared with increasing frequency in literature (Kubursi 2006; Zeitoun & Warner 2006a; Drake 2007; Gleick 1993; Lonergan 2001; Fisher n.d.; Sivakumar 2011; Benvenisti & Associa-2013)This literature often discusses various indicators for conflict, whether economical or ecological or social or even political. Yet despite the number of case studies little evidence have been provide of the relationship between freshwater and conflict. Nevertheless, the growing literature on trans-boundary water conflict, there is currently little empirical work being done to bolster any of the common conclusions being so widely reported.

- (Westing 1986) in his book Global resources and international conflict, suggests that "competition over scarce water resources leads to instigate political stress and may lead to war .
- (Gleick 1993)describes water resources as both (military and political) goals, using the case of Jordan
- (Zeitoun 2008)uses case studies from the Middle East of water as a cause of armed conflict;
- (Haftendorn 2000) write that deals with the origins of international conflicts over the use of rivers and ask what makes for a high conflict potential and whether there are significant differences between resource conflicts and conflicts arising

- (Shuval & Dweik 2007) argues that the Jordan and other water disputes, comes to the conclusion that the renewable resource most likely to stimulate interstate resource war.
- (Al-Kharabsheh & Ta'any 2005; Franklin M. Fisher 2002; Susskind & Shafiqul Islam 2013) argues for windows of opportunity and cooperation, they consider a radical way of thinking by shifting the consideration of water as a limited resources into the flexibility of water resources

All the mentioned above literature have many things in common which are;
- The use of inconsistent definitions. Terms as conflict, dispute, tensions are regularly used interchangeably
- Cooperation is left aside; the topic of concern is towards the water conflict and war as one of the main consequences, few of the literature mentioned points towards the attempts of cooperation(Susskind & Shafiq Islam 2013; Abukhater 2013); this could be mainly because most of the literature focuses on the hotspot areas from a political view.
- No concrete perception of the spatial scale and levels: the diversity of the parameters to measure water shortage, either per capita per sector. The parameters may also vary depending on the climate, population, water availability and accessibility, these multi scales are either ignored or fallen under the curse of generalizations.

The issues mentioned above drives the current study, pointing to the need reconsidered in my thesis: consistent and precise definitions of conflict and dispute; events along the entire spectrum of conflict and cooperation, the intensity of conflict; allowance for spatial variability, the applicability of water conflict literature over the Jordanian-Israeli water case.

Water among other issues as refugees and the status of Jerusalem had highly impacted the political agenda of the Jordanian-Israeli peace treaty, The research will attempt to analyze the water conflict resolution issues, starting from the cause of the conflict, which is water scarcity (by the assumption of the politicians of both sides), Building on the basic assumption that water has played and will play an important role in the Arab–Israeli conflict and its tentative resolution chapter, the research will examine the conflict development matter, and finally the research will dig deep in the resolution and negotiations approach, hence negotiation is a critical matter Governments consider when attempting to resolve or manage conflicts.

The research is much concerned with the understanding the fitness landscape of water conflict. It will also re-examine existing trans-boundary water conflict resolution theories, and establishing a new trend towards a future trans-boundary water conflict.

2.6. Research Structure:

The study will be structured into five chapters as explained in (Figure 1) :

Chapter one   Introduction , This chapter considers the general problem of trans-boundary conflict in protracted conflict settings by highlighting the landscape of conflict in the principal case study.

Chapter Two   Presents an overview of the theoretical considerations for the thesis. Research methodology and considerations.

Chapter Three This chapter will provide literature review and Theoretical framework, the chapter attempts to provide a theoretical foundation using theories of the relationship between science and politics, negotiation theory, conflict theory and complexity theory.

Chapter four This chapter will discuss the case study and set the scene for the bulk of the study by providing the background necessary for understanding the riparian conflict in the Jordan River basin and its relationship to the Arab-Israeli confrontation it will also walk the reader through the Water negotiations process, The historical analysis of the Israeli–Jordanian water negotiation process, it will also provide as Assessment of cooperation , delineates the profound resource constraints faced by Israel and Jordan, and outlines the various efforts the two states have made in recent years to develop domestic water supplies, We argue that just as the combination of resource need and relative power determines the possibility for cooperation in international river basins.

Chapter Five: This chapter weaves together the different threads of the research, drawing evidence from the empirical material of the case study by revisiting research questions, it will also discuss the lessons learnt from the case study.

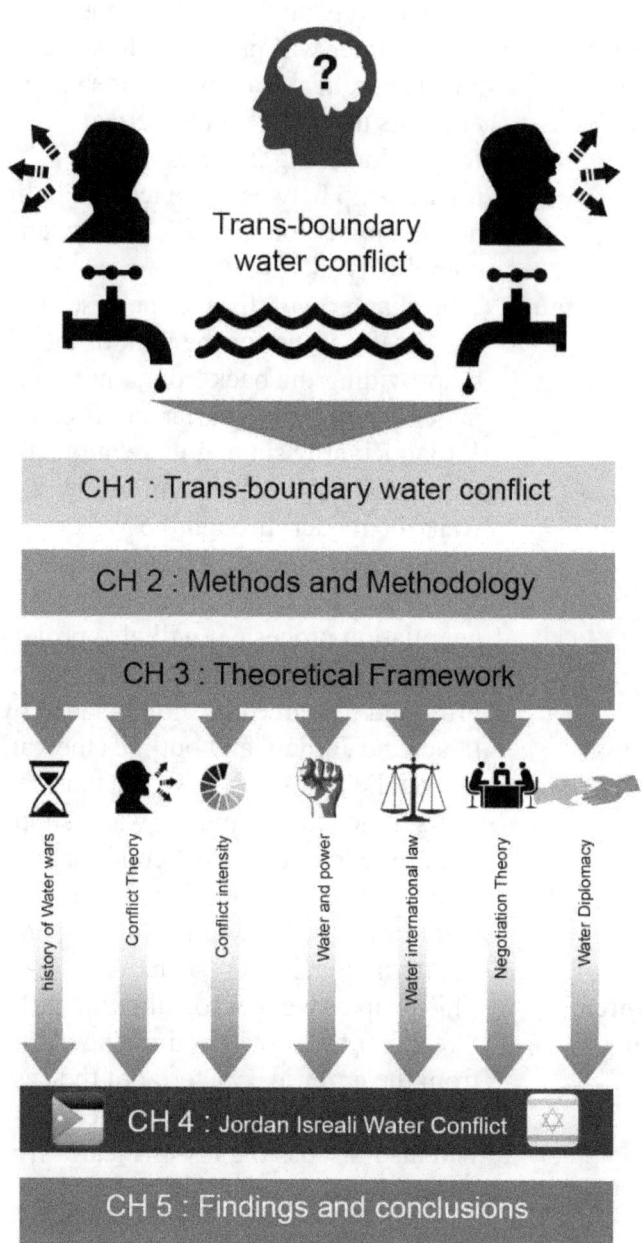

Figure 1: research road map, Source: Author

A number of indicators have been developed to measure each theory adopted in the understanding of the water conflict (see Table 1) , these indicators will be used later in chapter 4, to indicate the Jordan Israeli Water conflict

History of Water wars	Conflict Theory	Conflict intensity	Water and power	Water international law	Negotiation Theory	Water Diplomacy
The reality of water wars in history Water as a cause of war Water influence war	Conflict or dispute? Cause–effect relationships Systems and sub-systems are clearly bounded Easily predict the future.	Bar - 7/+7 Conflict intensity Cause and effect linkages are likely to be unclear	Power = Hydro-stability or Power = Hydro-hegemony Political factors	Willing to apply international law Resist international law The ability to force applying international law Who holds whom accountable Third Party involvement ARBITRATION	Bilateral Multilateral overcome deadlock Agreement among relevant stakeholders on means and ends is not hard to establish Joint problem-solving Bargaining or negotiation Holding on BATNA Steering	Joint fact finding Mutual Gains significant sensitivity New modes of operating and managing are likely to be required. water professionals are deeply cognizant of the network's initial configurations

						the network towards an agreed-upon future state Fair allocatio n Uncertai nty addresse d	Causes may not be proporti onal to effects, non-linear feedback Move toward the best possible solution space.

Table 1: Indicators of the criteria (Author)

This research is an inquiry into the conduct and resolution of conflicts over water resources in protracted conflict settings, by water conflict, *we refer "to a conflict among two or more sovereign states over access to or control over the water resources of an international river basin that traverses their territories"*(Lowi 2003), the main focus of the research is on the conflicts over shared water resources or trans-boundary waters that co-exist with a larger political conflict among the states in question.

The empirical material on which this inquiry is based, is drawn from the conflict over the waters of the Jordan River basin (see figure 2), an area which spans the territories of Israel, Jordan, Lebanon and Syria. This region has been the locus of an intense political conflict since the Arab defeat of war of 48 and the establishment of the state of Israel on the lands of Palestine (Kubursi 2006). The trans-boundary water conflict has been and continues to be an integral part of the protracted Arab-Israeli conflict.

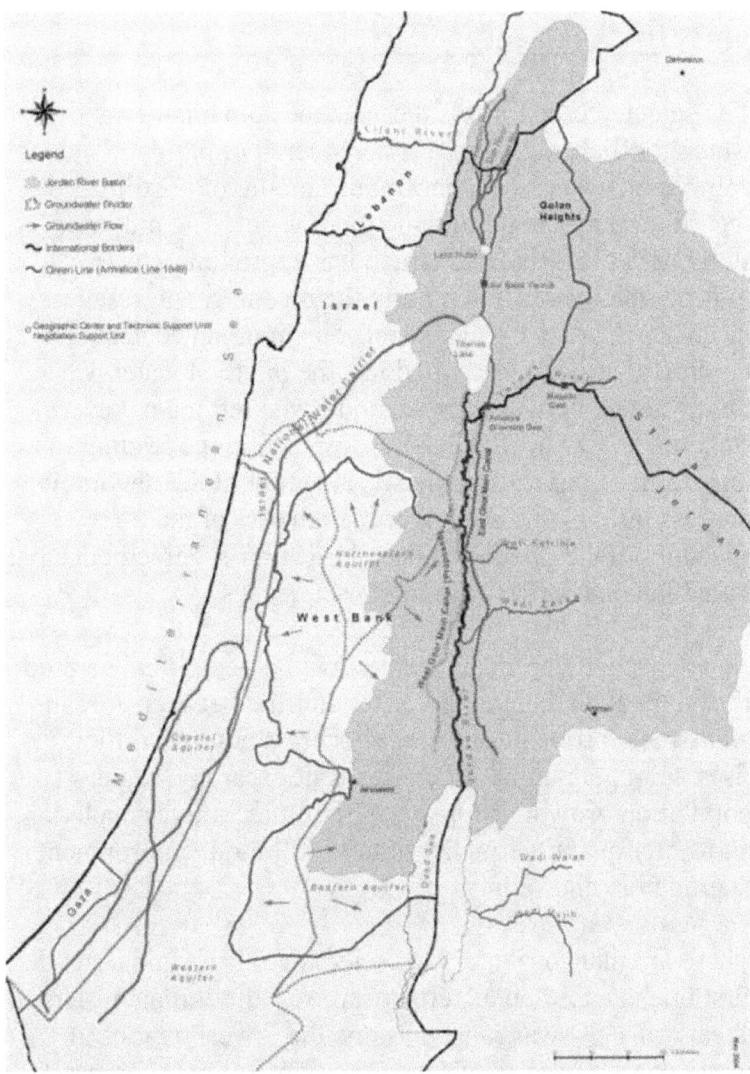

Figure 2: Jordan River Basin (Giordano et al. 2013)

1.1. The case Study:

The selected case for this thesis is the Jordanian-Israeli water conflict, as this area is considered of highly complexity issues with enormous amount of hostility regarding many issues among them water, The proposed study area of Jordan and Israel, has approximately 15 million inhabitants (exempting the recent Syrian refugees in Jordan), with varying proportions in urban centers and holding a variety of occupations. the bilateral water peace treaty signed between Jordan and Israel left many key stakeholders away, this lead and will continue leading to a long term of instability, the secret nature of the negotiation process left a dark space over the fairness of the treaty specially in the minds of many Jordanian's, agreements that failed to consider ecological consequences

To answer a theoretical question with an empirical method is of a great challenge, the water conflict between Jordan and Israel is a result of water allocation equity conflict, rises among a number of causes water scarcity, rapid population growth, extensive agriculture, aquifer depletion, and water quantity, quality issues, pollution, environmental degradation and salinity.

There are many criteria's for selecting this certain case: the first one is based on experts responses, the Jordanian-Israeli Treaty of 1994 was ranked as one the lowest treaties in terms of its perceived water allocation equity (Mirumachi & Nakayama 2007). This is because the treaty offers an example where lingering unresolved political issues, namely the Palestinian issue, greatly impacts both its outcome and perception. The second reason is the practical considerations or how old is the agreement and negotiation process, the case of the Jordanian-Israeli water conflict dates back to the 1994, and very recently in the November

2014 another cooperation treaty had been signed between *Jordanian-Israeli-Palestinian* parties regarding the Red Sea – Dead Sea water conveyor (Hazaimeh 2014). The third reason is related to the systematic review of literature and databases to verify and ensure the accuracy and consistency of the results, according to the (INTERNATIONAL TABULAR DATASETS)[1], Trans-boundary Freshwater Conflict Database (TFDD)[2], International Freshwater Treaties Database, International Water Events Database, Aquapedia, the Atlas of International Freshwater Agreements, emerged low on the term of fair water allocation.

1.2. Method of data and information collection:

I have been collecting the material for the research since 2007, the issue of water is one of my addictions, the first time I got truly involved in water issues was in year 2007 working as a team member of planners on the Jordan valley project which included the Red Sea-Dead Sea water conveyor as one of its components, I had a task at that time to collect several data from a wide spectrum of resources, from ministries and independent organizations. I have also used newspaper reports, Internet sources, various official documents and conducted personal interviews.

---

[1] http://www.transboundarywaters.orst.edu/database/

[2] The Middle East Water Collection is composed of approximately 9000 records pertinent to a variety of water issues in the Middle East. It provides materials such as data, books, journal and newspaper articles, and documents published in the Middle East, Europe, and North America political, socio-economic, demographic, and legal issues

Interviews have been an important method of data/information collection, interviews serve as an important way to test hypotheses and tentative conclusions, interviews are believed to be particularly useful since the research is concerned with a recent and ongoing process. This means that the stories that are told by the guests experience are fresh and dated.

An in-depth semi-structured interview (Annex B), has been designed as they have the possibility to 'steer' the interviews while at the same time allowing the respondents to elaborate where he/she feels it necessary to do so.

The respondents were identified according to three important criteria: find the people who have been most prominent in the negotiations and the implementation process:

1. Negotiators
2. Water experts and researches
3. Officials and ex-ministers of water and irrigations

1.3. Research challenges and limitations

This research does not include technical solutions. While engineering, hydrologic, or organizational aspects are extremely important, it seems that the problems of freshwater conflict resolution are superseded by constraints related to negotiating process by the sovereign stakeholder. The focus of the Thesis is more on political and social aspects, and the skills for conflict resolution. As Delli Priscoli (1989) explains, engineers and scientists need to expand beyond analytic solutions to water resources by adding techniques taken from the social sciences that are designed to facilitate reaching agreement, negotiators become more as facilitators who can bridge the gap between instrumental rational and social communicative rational.

To a large extent, attempts to simplify the theories of the classical theorists who argued about the shared resources are justifiable because their masterpieces are both works of science and works of art and their scientific core can be distilled into simple causal statements. Still, this approach may offend some readers by omitting much of the genius of the masters. Another problem is that simplified theories turn their back to some of the considerations mentioned by contemporary writers. For example, we do not include intervention by third parties as a part of our general theory, even though such interventions may affect the conflict in important ways. Thus this thesis should be viewed as only an attempt to synthesis the thesis and antithesis of trans-boundary water conflict between the state of Israel and the Kingdom of Jordan, one that deals just with the most important causes of conflict, and the process of conflict resolution.

3. Chapter Three
Theoretical Framework

3.1 Introduction

The question that concerns me here, though, is how trans-
boundary water conflict can be explained, These problems
each have their own particular causes, of course, and their
own unique casts of characters, Empirical work always
carries sacrificing analysis for detail by often leaving the
big questions unanswered, even ignored in some cases.
The question would still remain of what can be identified as
the general causes of water conflict among Jordan and
Israel, in trying to answer such a broad questions, this
chapter develops an analytical framework for explaining
trans-boundary water conflict. My aim here is not to
provide firm answers, but to clarify the terms of the
question, and to articulate some of the conflicting ways in
which water conflicts can be understood.

Water conflict resolution has identified itself as interdisciplinary; however, this term in my view, had failed to
achieve the potential and goals its terminology implies
within. We need a method that bridges and integrates the
gap between the theoretical and practical levels and it is
possible that trans-disciplinarily could spur this
development within the peace/conflict field.

The purpose of this chapter is to review the literature on
water conflicts and related water treaties to gain an
understanding of why water related conflicts have occurred.
This chapter presents the theoretical framework used in the
thesis. The theoretical ideas outlined in this chapter are
mainly used for the analysis made in coming chapters. The
present chapter is comparison between the conventional
water conflict resolution theories and the water diplomacy
framework theory.

Starting from the BIG picture, at the international level in an attempt to address international deficiencies several researches have argued that international agencies in several cases played a greater institutional role. (Dinar & Lee 1995) emphasized on the importance of an; integrated approach towards riparian basin planning, development, and management. (Harding et al. 1999) provided a number of guidelines for coordination among levels of management, starting at the global scale, to the national, regional, and ending with local levels. (Priscoli & Wolf 2008) (Fiadjoe 2004) emphasized on the role of public participation in water conflict management and they made a strong case for the potential of what they named as "Alternative Conflict Resolution" or (ADR). (Priscoli 1996) in the World Bank's handling of water resources issues. (Trolldalen 1997) in his article "Troubled Waters in Middle East" pointed out the complexity of water issues once merged into a political tense milieu accelerated by on ground growth problems whether these problems diverged from population growth or economic growth. Most recently, the water diplomacy framework established by Shafiqul Islam and Lawrence E. Susskind (2013) adapting complexity theory through negotiation in order to address uncertainties and build a water consensus.

3.2 Theoretical context:

This research draws upon a set of literature which focuses on the causes of conflict vs. the possibilities to cooperation, in answering how Trans-boundary waters; are managed through institutions and law. The section dealing with negotiation theory broadly examines the diagnosis of conflict, the prognosis or resolution, and presents some analysis on the case of Jordan-Israeli water conflict, It should be noted that most of the literature are in the context of arid regions including but not limited to the Middle East and the case of the Jordanian-Israeli water conflict.

This part serves as a theoretical underpinning for the thesis by outlining research approach and scholarly contribution in light of a critical evaluation and interpretation of the relevant literature. It provides an overview and analysis of the different bodies of literature that tackle the issue of water scarcity and conflict resolution in general and equitable allocation concepts and measurements in particular.

This research draws upon a set of literature which focuses on several aspects of the issue:
- Theory of conflict
- Water, and power (hydro-politics)(hydro-stability)(hydro-hegemony);
- Water international law;
- Negotiation theory
- Water diplomacy theory, as a window for the future

3.3 Defining the terms Conflict and Dispute:

The word 'conflict' is derived from two Latin words Con which means (together) and filigree (to strike), conflict entails a 'fight, struggle, collision'. Some of its synonyms are belligerency, hostilities, strife, war or clash, contention, difficulty, disdain, dissension, dissent, friction and strife. Additionally, conflict has been defined to include a clash of opposed principles, statements or arguments. (Fiadjoe 2004)

Literature review has revealed that, the terms conflict and dispute are used interchangeably without clear indication of the precise meaning of each other; many scholars and experts make a point to differentiate between the two terms, It is for this reason that, the term conflict has a wide range of definitions depends on the field it derived from. The Free dictionary, defines conflict as:

"A state of opposition, disagreement, or incompatibility between persons or a group of persons over ideas, interests, beliefs, feelings, behavior or goals."

Bartos and Wehr (Bartos & Wehr 2002)defines conflict as:

"Actors use conflict behavior against each other to attain incompatible goals and/or to express their hostility"

Brown and Marriot (1993) have a similar notion about conflicts.
"A conflict exists in the mind of an individual when [s]he perceives a situation of incompatibility among objectives. On the other hand dispute as a conflict in which both parties are conscious of."

whilst there is little consensus among sociological schools on a specific definition of conflict, a common denominator is that, for a conflict to occur, there must be an incompatibility of need and a perception by one party that this incompatibility interferes with the attainment of that person's needs.

In summary, their definition is illustrated in a diagrammatic form as a spectrum of conflict as shown in figure

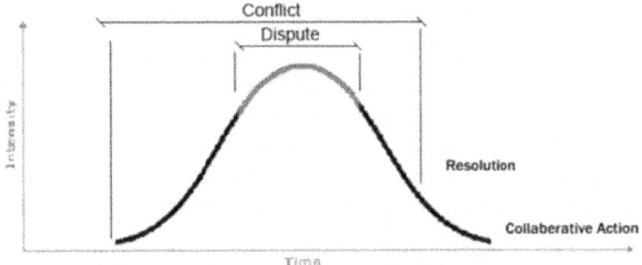

Figure 3: The Spectrum of Conflict Source: Author

For a clearer understanding of the difference between the two terms, a comparison between the characteristics of the meaning of conflict and dispute have been structured in (Table 2):

Conflict
- Long-term
- deep-rooted problems
- negotiation is the window opportunity
- Hard to negotiate
- possible to find a solution
- deep-rooted moral or value differences

Dispute
- Peak point of conflict
- Confrontation
- violent
- Short Term
- non-negotiable
- hard to find a solution
- incident
- confrontation

Table 2: a comparison in the meaning difference between conflict and dispute, Source: Author

While conflict is inevitable, disputes need not be. A conflict results in a dispute when technique of resolving the conflict are lacked (Fiadjoe 2004). The conventional classic responses to conflict is to fight over it, coerce or force a solution, it's more a game of win and lose or Zero sum solutions. The more powerful political party will always emerge as the winner. A diagrammatic representation of the causes of conflict is reproduced in the table 3.

41

42

Causes of conflict		
Different values	Unmet basic needs	Limited resources
Beliefs	*Power*	*Property*
Convictions	*Belonging*	*Money*
Principles	*Freedom*	*Time*
Priorities	*Funs*	*Natural Resources*

Table 3: origins of conflict source: (Fiadjoe 2004)

3.4 Conflict Theory:

Conflicts are processes, a chain of events that evolve through time and reshape. They are complex systems, one of the reason is that they intertwining into the context of our actions. Analyzing the conflict process, conflicts can be mapped and analyzed by a number of phases which are called in a number of literatures by "conflict life cycle" . There are distinct stages which conflicts have in common, in most cases conflict are close to chain reaction, through which they pass, sometimes they repeat themselves occasionally. studying the conflict life cycle models can be a helpful tool in understanding conflict in general, nevertheless water conflict follows a different path, as water conflict turn to fluctuate and depend on a number of factors, the conflict life cycle may not be a helpful tool to reflex upon.

Conflict defined as the existence of competing interests between states in absence of a shared interests, is an anomaly in international relations where the defining feature of the relationship between states is mutual dependence. The conflict over trans-boundary water resources is one of the major conflicts among states.

The main reason for establishing conflict over water comes of the main two properties of water the first one is its highly subtractive nature, and the second reason driver from the inability to exclude one party from utilizing it. Many political decision making mind consider water as a scare resources rather than a flexible one. Shafiqul Islam and Lawrence(Susskind & Shafiq Islam 2013) state that trans-boundary water conflict arise when:

1. a downstream party is worried that it won't have enough water during the dry season, or that it will experience flooding during the rainy season;
2. Parties have opposing perspectives regarding the emphasis that should be attached to ecological, economic, or equity considerations in the allocation or use of water;
3. Changes in the economic or demographic situation have led to rapidly growing demand for water;
4. Existing water allocation agreements appear to be causing water scarcity for some, resulting in substantial price increases;
5. Border conflicts arise between government entities or parties that favor one use (e.g., agriculture) as compared to another (e.g., tourism);
6. Threats to fishing downstream arise when pollution upstream creates water quality problems; and
7. Political entities each feel they have the authority to set new rules regarding the use or re-use of water supplies.

Deciding who will be getting waters, and for what reason always involves a huge challenge, such challenges can either be framed as a choice about who wins or loses, or can be recast as problems that need to be solved jointly (Shuval 2011)

The nature of water conflict are emergent and differs from time to time, depending on the context. Natural fluctuations in the available quantity of water, or shifting demand caused by changes in population increase or economic growth, can alter the nature of an allocation conflict or create a new one (Guan & Hubacek 2007)

When water conflicts involve sovereign nations, negotiations aimed at creating value are more complicated. Diverse national interests, cultural imperatives, and internal political demands usually lead to efforts to protect sovereignty at all costs. Water resource allocation problems within or between countries occur episodically, regardless of whether or not they are handled effectively when they first arise (Wolf 1995; Megdal 2007). Subsequent negotiations can become increasingly difficult when stakeholders have a history of past negotiations that deadlocked. Perceived injustices can also create some of the most vexing difficulties in later problem-solving efforts (Furlong and Gleditsch 2003; Dixit and Gyawali 2010). Competition for water at every level and in every domain will inevitably lead to conflict. Water managers and stakeholders can approach such conflicts using traditional hard-bargaining techniques, or they can adopt a non-zero-sum approach that emphasizes problem-solving and value creation through technology innovation, reframing, and trades of all kinds(Susskind & Shafiq Islam 2013).

		Ability to adopt and cooperate	
		Low	High
Availability of water	Scarce	Water Conflict	Structurally induced water abundance
	Abundant	Structurally induced water scarcity	Water Security

Table 4: Source: Redrawn from Ashton 2002

A comparison of the likely outcomes of societies with two levels of 'second-order resources' (i.e. social adaptive capacity) having to deal with two levels of first-order resources' (i.e. water abundance or water scarcity).

3.5 Water War Peace Rhetoric's;

Water has been frequently utilized as an effective weapon by riparian states to direct negotiations with others for the benefit of one powerful state(Lowi 2003). When countries share parts of a riparian basin, they tend to either cooperate or clash. By considering the two opposing schools of thought concerning conflict over water resources. A first school of thought has maintained since the 80's that competition over water will lead to wars as relative water scarcity increases around the planet. A second school of thought has emerged as a response, arguing that competition for water, far from leading states to wage war on each other, will rather incite them to cooperate (Trottier & Slack 2004).

Water conflicts will cause the wars of the future. This is statement made by many researchers and politicians, it is the object of numerous arguments and counter-arguments in the scientific community as much effort has been devoted to either proving or disproving the causal connection between water scarcity and water wars (Trottier & Slack 2004).

Since 1918 water has played a role only in initiating armed or near armed skirmishes between states. There have been only seven such recorded incidents. Not surprisingly, the majority of these episodes has taken place in the Middle East were water is scarce and the political atmosphere tense. (Velma I. Grover 2007)

According to(Gleick 1993), states that utilize the water as a weapon "water hegemony" (by restricting water flow to other states for political and military ends) may succeed in attaining and maintaining uninterrupted access to water resources, but their action tends to invoke violence. Opting to utilize water as a mean of threatening to influence and pressure other riparian states tends to exacerbate the problem, deepen the political divide and threaten the regional stability (Lowi 2003)

The Six-Day War also known in Hebrew by Milhemet Sheshet Ha Yamim and Naksah in Arabic (between Israel and Syria, Jordan and Egypt), the Israeli Prime Minister Levi Eshkol stated that "water is a question of survival for Israel," and that "Israel will use all means necessary to secure that the water continues to flow" (Benvenisti 2004), Commenting on the same event of the 1967 Six-Day War, the Crown Prince Hassan of Jordan stated that the war of 1967 "was brought on very largely over water related matters" and predicted that without an international water agreement in the Middle East by 2000 "countries in the region will be forced into conflict" (Wardam 2004). However, some researches claim that the main reason for the Six-Day war was not water. Haddadin (2002) states that; the main reason was PLO guerrillas attacking Israel through the Israeli Syrian boarders, this last statement challenges the prediction of a future war over water distribution.

Close examination of the water war claims in the media and the actual observation of the number of times there is real violence over water, reveals that the occurrences of violence are quite few as compared with the number of treaties signed for cooperation among countries sharing water. (Sivakumar 2011)

A second school of thought emerged during the 1990's, denying the causality between water scarcity and international war. The concept of cooperation over water conflict is not new, it goes back to the early ages; In Old Testament times; there were two ways of solving conflicts over water, even at that time water was considered a scarce resource. One way was to fight over it. The other was to jointly place over the mouth of the well a large stone so that five of the strongest shepherds were needed to lift it, each shepherd from a different clan. Creating the need for cooperation. "Israeli Agriculture Minister Yaacov Tsur" (Bard 2007)

After signing a peace agreement with Israel in 1979, Egyptian President Anwar Sadat announced that the only issue that would prompt Egypt to declare war again would be water (Velma I. Grover 2007)

To argue that conflict is an anomaly in the realm of hydro-politics would be a distortion of reality (Velma I. Grover 2007). A re-examination of the water-war literature reveals that. The existing body of literature on water and conflict in the Middle East has focused on the power of states while ignoring the cooperation among states and institutions that participated in controlling water management, a new investigative framework needs to be designed that will allow us to explore conflict dynamics beyond interstate war.

Water-related conflicts ensue as a result of resource scarcity and access limitation, coupled with population growth. Because of population growth and resource limitation, conflict over the quantity and quality of water access will often occur creating a situation of hostility. This illustrates the potential conflictive nature of trans-boundary water if not properly managed through cooperative arrangements among these rivals. Many scholars, such as (Fisher, et al., 2001; Wolf, 1996; and M. J. Haddadin, 2002), argue that allocation of water resources should not be viewed as a catalyst for war, but rather an initiative for diplomacy and potential conflict resolution.

3.6 Conflict Intensity:

Aaron T. Wolf, Shira B. Yoffe and Mark Giordano (Wolf et al. 2003) have contributed to the field of measuring the water conflict intensity, the developed a tool called BAR, this tool is intended to aid the systematic assessment of the process of water conflict resolution, they have been working for many years to develop the Trans-boundary Freshwater Dispute Database (TFDD)[3], thorough this huge data the came up with a tool called BAS (basin at risk), BAS is a scale from -7 to 7 the -7 is the most intense situation that leads to war, while 7 is the least intense. The scale is more elaborated in the Table 4 & 5.

The purpose of their analysis is to enrich the debate on trans-boundary water conflicts in an attempt to shed light over cardinal questions; who gets how much quantity of the water, how and why? It will be argued that control over water resources is not achieved through water wars but through a suite of power-related and hegemonic tactics and strategies (Yoffe et al. 2003).

BAR scale	BAR event description
−7	Formal declaration of war; extensive war acts causing deaths,
−6	dislocation or high strategic costs
-5	Extensive military acts
	Small scale military acts
-4	Political–military hostile actions
-3	Diplomatic–economic hostile actions
-2	Strong verbal expressions displaying hostility in interaction
-1	Mild verbal expressions displaying discord in interaction
	Neutral or non-significant acts for the inter-nation situation
0	Minor official exchanges, talks or policy expressions—mild verbal

[3] This database includes: a digital map of the world's 263 international watersheds; a searchable compilation of 400 water-related treaties, the data base includes of international water-related disputes and dispute resolution (1948–2000)

1	support
2	Official verbal support of goals, values or regime
3	Cultural or scientific agreement or support (non-strategic)
4	Non-military economic, technological or industrial agreement
5	Military economic or strategic support
6	International freshwater treaty; major strategic alliance (regional or international)
7	Voluntary unification into one nation

Table 5: BAR Event intensity scale. (Wolf et al. 2003)

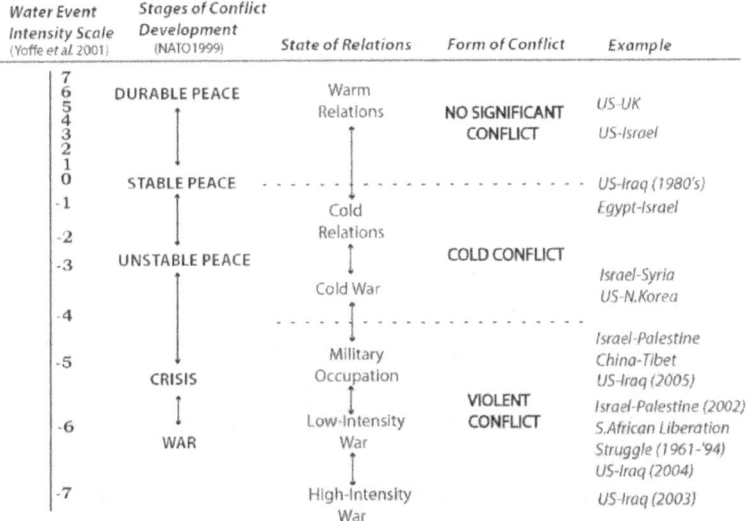

Table 6: Conflict Intensity Frame. (Zeitoun & Warner 2006b)

Overall distribution of events over the 50-year period of assessment, there was no water event to be graded on the extreme scale of -7, that mean no war was ever erupted for the sake of waters alone. The second very interesting findings was the Most interactions are cooperative, Cooperative events are more than twice as common as conflictive events, the third finding was that only 50 % of the cases fallen between -2 (official verbal hostility) to

+2(Official verbal support), the study carried by Wolf, Shira, Yoffe and Giordano is a strong supportive evidence that cooperation is more likely to happen that war.

One way of mapping and analyzing water conflict is to think of the conditions surrounding a water network as "fitness landscape", defining the fitness landscape is the main tool towards building a consensus over issues while at the same time addressing uncertainty, mapping the nodes and the interactions among them would establish the fitness landscape of the water conflict arena of conflict, Of course, what constitutes "fitness" is likely to change over time.

3.7 Water and power:

Water has been considered the flows of power (Swyngedouw 2008). Political science teaches us that power is always at work, and is always contestable; Power also determines who is in control. With conflict and power the concept of hegemony provides a means of analyzing and communicating about international power imbalances. Shafiqul Islam and Susskind discussed that within the natural domain, the interplay among three important variables, water quantity (Q), water quality (P), and ecosystems (E) can lead to conflict. Within the societal domain, there are equally complex interdependencies and feedback among social values and cultural norms (V), assets including economic and human resources (C), and governance institutions (G) (Islam, et al 2010; Islam and Susskind 2011).

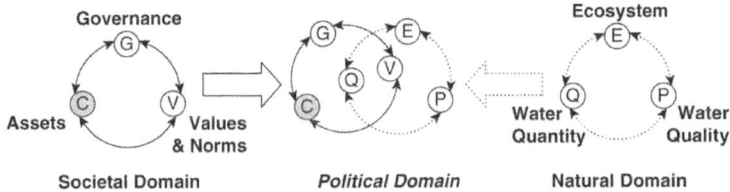

Figure 4 Interactions among natural and societal
processes within a political domain (Susskind & Shafiqul
Islam 2013)

Societal domain and Natural domain are interacted by
the power of the political domain, political domain forms
the fuzzy area or the interface among the two domains and
creates the rules of engagement. The need to integrate
across these three domains has been recognized by many
other water scholars and practitioners (Pahl-wostl et al.
2007; Lankford & Cour 2005)(Biswas 1994). Understating
the interaction among these three domains will pave the
road for a more efficient solvable conflict over trans-
boundary water resources, especially when data are
difficult to collect and not readily comparable because of
disparities in scales and levels, or even the attempts to
misinform.

In the case of trans-boundary water conflicts the
political domain is presented in the power of the state
which come in three shapes (hydro-Hegemony) (hydro-
dependency) and (hydro-stability), this creates a new
window to look over the issue, the encounter between states
will be among the political domains of each state, as water
in many cases is considered one of the pillars of the state
sovereignty, power imbalances reveal to the surface
(Swyngedouw 2005), and power imbalance could be
revealed in the form of hydro-hegemony. Hydro-
hegemonies have the option to write the agenda for all this
riparian contestation.

Hydro-hegemony is a mix between force and consent, it's a way to decide 'who gets to say what', effectively setting the agenda at the exclusion of the consideration of alternatives, Power asymmetries that clearly advantage the ability to influence one riparian actor (states, in our case) over others (Zeitoun & Warner 2006b), Negative and dominative hegemonic behavior results in an ever-growing inequity between the powerful and the weak within the hydro-political domain,

The table below helps clarifying the political domain and the hydro-politics approaches appropriate to different water conflicts.

Base of Conflict	Example
Control of Water Resources where water supplies or access to water is at the root of the tensions	Egypt-Sudan 1958; Israel-Syria 1958; Brazil-Paraguay 1979.
Water as a Political Tool	Iraq-Syria 1974; Turkey-

where water resources or water systems are used by a nation, State or non- State actor for a political goal.	Syria-Iraq 1990; Malaysia-Singapore 1997
Water as a Tool for Terrorism where water resources, or water systems are used by a non-State actor as tools of violence or coercion.	East Timor 1999; Kosovo 1999; Israel, Palestine 2001; Nepal 2002; US-Iraq 2003.
Water as a Military Tool where water resources, or water systems themselves, are used by a nation or State as a weapon during a military action.	Ethiopia-Somalia 1948; Israel-Lebanon 1982; Bosnia 1992; Kosovo 1999; US-Iraq 2003
Water as a Military Target where water resource systems are targets of military actions by nations or States.	Israel-Syria 1967; Israel-Jordan 1969; South Africa-Angola 1988; US-Afghanistan 2001.
Development Conflicts where water resources or water systems are a major source of contention and conflict in the context of economic and social development.	Ethiopia-Somalia 1963; Bangladesh 1999; Pakistan 2001; Turkey-Syria-Iraq 1990.

Table 7 : base of conflict, (Zeitoun & Elisa 2010)

To further understand the role of power in shaping the hydro-politics a thorough look over the work of Zeitoun and Elisa helps a lot. Mark Zeitoun and Ana Elisa (2010) articulated a new 'hydro-politics' framework for the analysis of trans-boundary water politics, (Zeitoun & Elisa

2010) argue that conventional analyses tend to underestimate the importance of power in water conflict, and that further attention is needed to understand the dynamics of power over water, Zeitoun & Warner (2006b) observed that the feared threat of 'water wars' is 'non-existent', and that trans-boundary cooperation has been much the more widespread feature of international water politics. they argue, the attempt to control trans-boundary water resources can take place through a number of power tactics, ranging from military force at one extreme, to the agreement of unequal water treaties. Within the context of power asymmetrical, the distribution of water resources is largely determined by the hydro-hegemonic power (Selby 2007).

Zeitoun and Elisa (2010) divide power into four forms; Geographical power, Material power, Bargaining power, Ideational power. Geographical power: relies on the distinct advantage that geography provides to an upstream state to manipulate the flows, however, shows that geographic position can be less influential and determining than other fields of power. Material power: This most visible form of power includes economic power, military might, technological prowess and international political and financial support. Bargaining power. This field of power refers to the capability of actors to control the rules of the game and set agendas, in the sense of their ability to define the political parameters of an agenda, It is also evident in the power of actors to influence the terms of negotiations and agreements. The fourth and final form of power is Ideational power. This dimension refers to 'power over ideas' Lukes (1974) which represents the capacity of a riparian to impose and legitimize particular ideas and narratives. In sum, ideational power allows the basin hegemon to control the perceptions of the water allocation of the societies both in its own country and in the neighboring riparian countries, thereby reinforcing its legitimacy. Hegemonic state may manipulate the interaction with the other state through a number of tools, including lack of knowledge and data sharing, or the use of time, silence or ambiguity(Hajer 1997). (Ex. A refusal by the Israeli side to share data on water use(Zeitoun & Elisa 2010, World Bank, 2009)). A quick glance at Figure below explains the four pillars or forms of power.

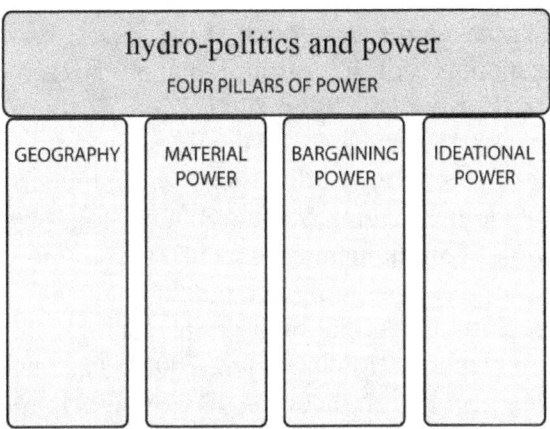

Figure 5: forms of power (Zeitoun & Elisa 2010)
modified by author

This section has demonstrated the merit in viewing trans-boundary contexts through a lens of critical hydro-politics. The testing of the theory will be detailed in the coming chapter

3.1 Negotiation Theory:

Negotiation is a process of defining and reducing alternative positions through building a unique alternative that is accepted by all parties; it is a collective decision-making process (Rossi 1958).

Negotiation is a vehicle of communication, in many Trans-boundary water conflicts; stability is achieved by conflict management, negotiation theory fall very handy in understanding a conflict resolution and management. As Zartman (Zartman & Rubin 2002; I. W. Zartman 2001; Zartman 2001; Zartman 1975) defines Negotiation is the process of combining of divergent/conflicting positions through communication into a joint decision. Negotiation is any form of communication between two or more people for the purpose of arriving at a mutually agreeable solution (Fiadjoe 2004). Negotiation is an increasingly important policymaking tool (Rachael et al. 2008). The reason for including negotiation theory is that it will help to reveal the influence perceptions of water have had in favor of the resolution of the conflict or its continuation. Negotiation theories may be prescriptive, descriptive, or normative in nature. practitioners have developed and utilized a variety of approaches or to improve their understanding of particular aspects of negotiations. Negotiation is an exchanging act; means giving something to get something. Negotiations are presumed to be an important tool for the establishment of water regimes, which are a central theme of this thesis.

To understand the applicability of negotiation theory we have to examine the diagram (Figure 6), as it shows that in reality conflicts are due to two major factors that are Goals and Instruments, Goals represent the main values behind the conflict while instruments are representatives of tools, methods and knowledge, negotiations accrue when there is an agreed goals among the parties but there is a dissensus on the instruments. Water trans-boundary conflict is of no exclusion, parties agreed on the importance to reach agreements but are still in doubts on how and when.

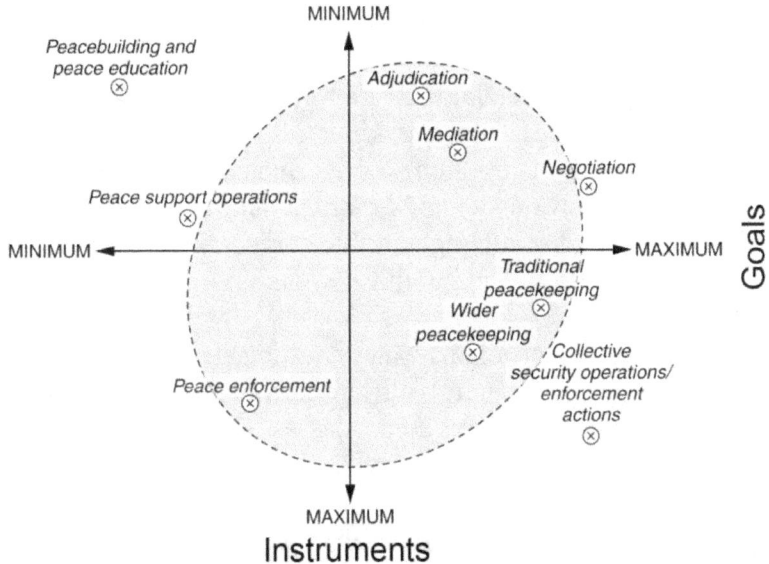

Figure 6: Conflict management: plotting the points (Butler 2009) modified by author

Trans-boundary waters are different even, non-comparable because water resource endowments, terrain and, even more important, institutional infrastructures are everywhere different (Zeitoun & Allan 2008). According to Gert De Roo (Roo & Silva 2010) and Horst Rittel (Rittel & Webber 1973) it is important to distinguish between three types of problems: simple, complicated, and complex. This classification can be applied to water problems as well, Simple problems are characterized as easily comprehendible, while complicated problems are harder to solve, but still are knowable and predictable. On the other hand Complex problems, are problems formed with high uncertainty and unpredictable.

Many of our contemporary water problems can be categorized under complex problems, and we cannot talk about finding optimal or engineered solutions unless a great many non-objective assumptions are imposed. These subjective considerations undermine the credibility of water managers who claim they are relying on purely scientific or technical judgments (Susskind & Shafiqul Islam 2013). Water conflicts might be more effectively managed or resolved if we understood more about the interaction and feedback loops among variable components of the relevant natural, societal, and political systems.

The kinds of problems water conflicts deal with societal problems are inherently different from the problems that scientists and perhaps some classes of engineers deal with. Water conflicts are inherently wicked. The role of scientific data in trans-boundary conflict is to build an advocacy data in order to gain trust, rather than brokering data for parties.

When water conflicts cross national borders, negotiated solutions are the only option since sovereign nations cannot be forced to accept terms to which they object(Susskind & Shafiq Islam 2013). As stated by Saeb Erekat (Palestinian chief negotiator)(2008 عريقات), in his book a life of negotiation, who could ever imagined that the German counselor would give a speech at the Israeli Knesset, or who could ever imagined that the NATO summit would be held in Bucharest[4]. It's apparently the mystic effect of negotiation than can overcome any kind of conflict.

---

[4] *Bucharest after being considered one of the Warsaw coalition hearts*

Negotiation theory emphases that in international conflict two forms of negotiation arises one is a bilateral approach, the other is multilateral approach, negotiation theory literature emphasizes of the first approach, negotiations are almost exclusively bilateral, whereas multilateral negotiations are above all matters of coalition, (Table 8) below describes the characteristic of each approach.

Bilateral	Multilateral
standing firm	Justification
subordination	Cooperation
power assertion:	Coalition
verbal/physical	Integrative /
coercion	granting appeals
Bargaining	compromise
Dividing	Sharing
separation	Conciliation/
avoidance/withdrawal	continued interaction
	peaceful reunion

Table 8: Characteristics of Bilateral and Multilateral negotiations

BATNAs (Best Alternative to a Negotiated Agreement) can be an important source of power or strength in a negotiation. A more 'powerful' party with a weaker BATNA will need to come to a negotiated agreement more than its rival. A BATNA provides negotiators with a measure of flexibility, For this reason, Fisher and Ury (Fisher & Ury 1991)maintain that developing a BATNA can be the best tool when facing powerful negotiators.

A dominant assumption in water management has been that the allocation of common resources, is always a win–lose situation, Actor with more power "win" and gain control of resources, less powerful parties "lose" the access to water is only permitted by the will of the party with more power (Susskind & Shafiqul Islam 2013) (Abukhater 2013). The emergence of non-zero-sum, or mutual gains negotiation theory, over the past few decades, has challenged this win–lose logic by offering a "value-creating" alternative that allows groups with conflicting goals to achieve them simultaneously (Schelling 1957; Gullickson & Ramser 1996; Crump 2011; Raiffa 1982). This mutual gains approach to negotiation rests on the assumption that joint fact-finding, the discovery of interlocking trades, contingent commitments, and an adaptive approach to handling uncertainty can maximize joint gains (MJG). "Coordinated interests" negotiations usually require the assistance of a facilitator or mediator who is ethically neutral to manage the process of joint problem solving (Susskind and Cruikshank 1987).

3.1.1 Stages of Negotiation:

As Mediators (Third Party) appears in all the Arab-Israeli conflict, we will discuss the three stages of negotiation were mediator is involved and presented in each and every stage.

Negotiation moves through three stages, the first stage is referred to by the pre-negotiation stage, the intention behind this stage is often 'talks about talks' or 'getting to the table'. This stage sets the structure of the negotiations and paves the road towards the upcoming stages, as this stage has no commitment body, it builds the bridges of trust among the parties and defines the real problems and ratifies skeptical questions, the role of a mediator is major at this stage as he/she helps in overcoming the face to face communication, and creates a more rational discussions by guaranteeing equal access to every party

The second stage in the negotiation stage, this stage is marked by the signing of the agreement, at this stage issues are clarified and deals are made, mediator will give his blessing to the parties and new common ground is established by identifying a mutually accepted agreement, Negotiation can be approached in many ways. Whatever the strategy chosen, success lies in how well prepared. The key to negotiating a beneficial outcome is the negotiators' ability to consider carefully all the elements of the situation and to identify and think through the alternatives and possibilities.

The Third and final stage is called the Post-Negotiation stage, the stage of implementation where the treaty is been tested for applicability and the commitments of the signed parties to fulfill their agreed upon duties. Parties at this stage try to implement the agreement in reality, any delay in the implementation of the agreement will raise the contentions once again and could blow the whole agreement. This stage is highly critical in sustaining a long-term agreement

3.2 Water international law

The international law is a newly born law; it appeared only after the WWI (Guillermo J. Canoa 1989), The International Law Commission, a U.N. body, was directed by the General Assembly in 1970 to study "Codification of the Law on Water Courses for Purposes Other than Navigation." It is essential to mention that the total numbers of international water agreements that are force in the Middle East are five. Some of these treaties are devoted exclusively to water issues, while others deal with different water. Below are the treaties in place (Schiffler 1998):
- The Agreement on the Full Utilization of the Nile Waters, 8 November 1959;
- The Protocol of Economic Cooperation between Syria and Turkey, July 1987;
- The Jordanian-Syrian Agreement on the Utilization of the Waters of the Yarmuk River, 3 Sep 1987;

- The Syrian-Iraqi Agreement on the Utilization of the Euphrates Waters, April 1990;
- The Peace Treaty between Israel and Jordan, 26 October 1994.

Conflict over trans-boundary derives from the nature of the waters itself, as it is hardly impossible to draw a clear property lines this is also a cause of the vagueness of legal principles (Velma I. Grover 2007). International water treaty literature generally identifies two types of equity; distributive and procedural justice (Abukhater 2013). Procedural justice entails three accounts;

1. *perfect procedural justice*, with independent criteria of fairness and a procedure that guarantees fair outcomes,
2. *imperfect procedural justice*, with independent criteria of fairness but no method that guarantees fair outcomes, and
3. *pure procedural justice*, with neither.(Metz 2002)(Rawls 2001)

International water treaty literature indicates that common water allocation practice is based on either hydro- or geopolitical grounds (Doppler et al. 2002) the hydro-argument is relevant to the origin of a river or aquifer and how much of its boundary falls within each riparian state, This falls under two theories "Absolute territorial sovereignty theory" and the theory of "Absolute territorial integrity theory" which are opposite to each other. The doctrine of absolute territorial sovereignty argument is often made by upstream riparian's who claim, based on the Harmon Doctrine, "buried, not praised" absolute sovereignty of water falling in their boundary(Attila 2010). The three pronged pillar of International Water Law are:

(1) the equitable utilization,
(2) no-harm and

(3) Cooperation.

The principle states that an upstream state can essentially do what it wants regardless of harm to the downstream state. Conversely, the latter principle states that the downstream state has a right not to be harmed by the upstream state. The principle of equitable and reasonable utilization establishes that a state both has a right to utilize its waters in an equitable and reasonable manner and at the same time the duty to cooperate in the river's protection and development. In other words, a state has a right to an equitable and reasonable share in the beneficial uses of the waters of the basin, yet that the state should not use these waters in such a way as to unreasonably interfere with the legitimate interests of other states (Attila 2010)(Velma I. Grover 2007).

The 1997 Convention has stirred some controversy among states, which may favor one Article over another; it is important to note that it does not attempt to provide countries with specific guidelines for conflict resolution. Rather it attempts to codify customary law in the most general terms. (Velma I. Grover 2007). Property rights are essentially negotiated, and water treaty observations have made clear the ability of states to develop systems of property rights and liability rules in the absence of an overarching international body. As such, cooperation and negotiation are scrutinized next.

One of the biggest burdens to water's role as a peace agent is the lack of an agreeable equity measure for dividing shared water resources (Wolf 1996). Analyzing international water agreements in middle east should be made by analyzing the below :
- Consideration of customary international law, in particular the 1997 United Nations Convention on

the Law of Non-navigational Uses of International Watercourses (referred to as the Water Convention) and the 1966 Helsinki Rules of the International Law Association (lLA);

- Consideration of the water rights of other riparian states located on a river, which are not signatories of international water agreements;
- Distribution of the risk of low flow rates;
- Water quality and protection of wetlands;
- Elaboration of procedures and creation of commissions to monitor and enforce treaty provisions, and
- An implicit or explicit linkage of the water question with other (political) issues.

3.3 Water Diplomacy:

Water diplomacy approach might posit a more effective conflict resolution by balancing water asymmetries and rethinking water as a flexible resource and abandoning the traditional approach as water is scarce and limited, this requires laying a number of assumptions:

1. Water networks are flexible and continuously changing as a dynamism of the interactions among natural domain, societal domain, and political domain;
2. Water network must acknowledge uncertainty, nonlinearity, and feedback; and
3. The management approach of water networks should shift towards a more adaptive and negotiated considering a "non-zero-sum" approach.

The table below is a summary of the main differences between Water Network framework and conventional water conflict resolution theories

Water diplomacy framework theory	Conventional water conflict resolution theories
Water is a flexible resource Complexity Process optimization Non-zero sum Adaptive Context dependent	Water is at scarcity and a limited resource Simple to complicated Zero-sum Game-theory Static, linear One solution fits all

Table 9: how to differentiate between conventional water conflicts theories and water network theory

In order to understand the intricacies among the water network rational and the water system rational, the table below classifies the differences much clearly:

Criteria	The Water diplomacy	Conventional conflict water system resolution theory
Main Assumption	Water is a flexible resource	Water is a scarce resource
Domains and scales	Water crosses multiple domains (natural, societal, political)and boundaries at different scales (space, time, jurisdictional, institutional).	Watershed or river-basin falls within a bounded domain.
Water availability	Virtual waters, blue and green water, technology sharing and negotiated problem-solving that permit re-use can "create flexibility" in water for competing demands.	Water is a scarce resource; competing demands over limited resources will lead to conflict.
Water systems	Water networks are made up of societal and natural elements that cross boundaries and change constantly in unpredictable ways within a political context	Water systems are bounded by their natural components; cause–effect relationships are known and can be readily modeled.
Water management	All stakeholders need to be involved at every decision-making step including problem framing; heavy investments in experimentation and monitoring are key to adaptive management; the process of collaborative problem-solving needs to be professionally	Decisions are usually expert-driven; scientific analysis precedes participation by stakeholders; long-range plans guide short-term decisions; the goal is usually optimization, given competing political demands.

	facilitated.	
Key analytic tools	Stakeholder assessment, joint fact-finding, scenario planning and mediated problem-solving are the key tools.	Systems engineering, optimization, game theory, and negotiation support-systems are most important.
Negotiation theory	The Mutual Gains Approach (MGA) to value creation; multiparty negotiation keyed to coalitional behavior; mediation as informal problem-solving are vital to effective non-zero-sum negotiation	Hard bargaining informed by prisoner's dilemma-style game theory; principal–agent theory; decision-analysis (Pareto optimality); theory of two-level games.

Table 10: a comparison between water diplomacy framework and conventional water conflict resolution approaches **(Susskind & Shafiqul Islam 2013)** modified by author

Conventional approach's entail that specialist and experts highly rely on the ability to make forecasts and estimations for future requirement basing their calculation over historical data, this approach is a critical and dangerous approach and is based over an assumption that the forecasts will yield a clear pattern or tendency that can be relied on to occur. However, in the complex world of water management, there is too much uncertainty to forecast with confidence. The emergence of wars and enormous amount of refugee in Middle East, for example, has already altered the dynamics of the hydrologic cycle in Jordan, accordingly it is crucial that communities take action now to adapt to the changes and risks revealed. That does not mean that experts should stop calculating and generating estimations, on the contrary that requires experts to address uncertainty more clearly (Susskind & Shafiq Islam 2013).

There are tools for managing water resources while at the same time acknowledging uncertainty, these tools are quite different from the conventional modeling and forecasting tools that assume certain amounts of water flows that can be modeled with predictive accuracy (Abukhater 2013; Abukhater 2010).

In Trans-boundary waters, zero-sum thinking has a self-fulfilling quality. If water managers believe that supplies are limited, and that only some users will be able to use the water for what they want, then the potential "winners" act accordingly, and the result is inevitable. If the stakeholders in such situations set as their goal that they want to meet the objectives of almost all the relevant stakeholders simultaneously, can they always succeed? In theory, parties in water conflicts ought to be able to find ingenious ways of using the same water in a variety of ways, or of helping each other reduce their demand for water, so that the interests of all parties can be met. There are instances in practice of such "joint gains" being achieved. (Velma I. Grover 2007)(Susskind & Shafiq Islam 2013)

Trans-boundary water negotiation in many cases is unavoidable trap of zero-sum thinking, this is not necessarily easy to accomplish, and reaching equitable water agreements is not a piece of cake task. In many places around the world, water is still viewed as a scarce rather than a flexible resource. Fear about water scarcity makes value creation difficult. The key difference between a value-creating approach to negotiation and the traditional hard-bargaining approach is that parties invest time in "trying to make the pie as large as they can" before allocating gains and losses (Franklin M. Fisher 2002). By taking this approach, parties can move away from the zero-sum assumption that there is a fixed amount of water that has to be allocated to one side or the other, moving from a focus on "positions" or demands, to "interests," A value-creating approach to water negotiation also requires sharing rather than withholding information (Sadoff and Grey 2005). The whole process of negotiation may be summarized in moving from hard bargaining to collaborative problem-solving.

For problem-solving forums to succeed, the right parties need to be represented at the table. They need to agree on a negotiation agenda that incorporates the most important items of concern to all the parties, design and implement a joint fact finding process, and formulate mutually beneficial agreements.

Shafiqul and Lawrence explained a useful mechanism; they named it Joint Fact Finding process, (see Table 11). Most water problems involve numerous parties concerned about a variety of issues. The more the number of parties involved the more the situation gets messy and hard to negotiate, this requires limiting the number of stakeholders involved by attaining a stakeholder assessment. This emphasizes the importance of international water Consensus Building another Process that is explained in (Table 12). Highly complex decision making problems are suitable for consensus planning (Woltjer 2004). The way a stakeholder assessment works is that the convener makes an inventory of all the categories of stakeholders with concerns about whatever water management issue needs to be addressed. Then, the convener selects a facilitator to interview all the relevant individuals or groups in each category. Based on the responses, the facilitator makes a judgment about whether it makes sense to proceed given potential financial, institutional, and other constraints. If it does, the facilitator determines under what circumstances the stakeholders will agree to participate. Not only do stakeholder representatives have to be identified, but also experts who can ensure that the parties have the scientific, technical, and legal information they need. Generally, the facilitator talks to advocacy groups, community representatives, business leaders, and independent scientific experts. Based on the out-come of these conversations, the "neutral" proposes a work plan, timetable, ground rules, and budget. These are put in written form and sent to everyone interviewed to get their reactions and seek their endorsement. The strategy for joint fact-finding (JFF), and the identification of appropriate technical advisors is one of the products of the facilitator's conversations with all the parties.

Prepare	Scope	Define	Conduct the Study	Evaluate	Communicate
Understand how JFF fits into consensus building	Work with stakeholders to define responsibilities	Translate questions in researchable questions	Undertake the work checking back with constituents	Use sensitivity analysis to examine the overall significance of scientific assumptions and findings	Jointly present findings to stakeholders
Document interest of all stakeholders	Generate technical questions	Identify relevant methods of information gathering, and highlight the benefit's and disadvantages	Draw on expertise knowledge of stakeholders	Compare findings to published literature	Scientist communicate JFF results to various constituencies and policy makers
Work with professional neutrals	Identify existing information and knowledge gaps	Determine costs and benefits of alternatives information gathering	Review drafts of the final JFF	Clarify remaining uncertainties and appropriate contingent response	Determine if further JFF is necessary

				s
Convene a JFF process	Advise on methods for dealing with conflicting data and interpretations			Determine whether and how JFF results have answered questions

Table 11: Joint Fact Finding process

Convene	**Sign on**	**Deliberate**	**Decide**	**Implement agreements**
Initiate discussion	Specify roles and responsibilities of convener facilitator representatives and expert advisors	Strive for transparency	Seek unanimity on a package or proposal to maximize mutual gains	Seek ratification by constituencies
Prepare an issue assessment	Set rules for involvement of observers	Seek expert input into joint fact finding	Specify contingent commitments if appropriate	Present approved proposal to those with the formal authority and responsibility to act
Finalize commitments to consult or involve appropriate	Set rules for involving of others	Seek to maximize joint gains through collaborati	Adhere to agreed upon decision making	Provide for on-going monitoring

stakeholders representatives		ve problem solving	procedures	
Use the assessment to identify appropriate stakeholder representative	Assess options for communicating with parties	Use the help of neutral-professionals	Meeting should be Documented in written and signed by parties	Provide adaptive changing circumstances
Make sure the higher level of authority is aware of the process steps and contented with it.				

Table 12: consensus-building process (Susskind & Shafiq Islam 2013)

Lawrence Susskind has claimed (Susskind 1994) that At the present time, the basic structure of the United Nations approach towards water conflict resolution is its limited emphasis on national representation and the maintenance of sovereignty, works against these prerequisites previously mentioned, Global water treaty making and the international cooperation needed to implement effective treaties require extensive consensus building, which, in turn, requires effective ad hoc representation of all the stakeholders, face-to-face interaction among skilled representatives of the stakeholders interests, a real give-and-take aimed at maximizing joint gains, facilitation by appropriate neutral parties at various points in the process, informality that allows the parties to speak their minds, and extensive pre-negotiation that ensures opportunities for joint problem solving. It is important to be aware of what will happen if there is no agreement. In preparing for any water management negotiation, it is important to estimate one's BATNA (best alternative to a negotiated agreement), If there are only two parties involved in a negotiation, there are only two BATNAs to consider in determining whether there is a likely zone of possible agreement (ZOPA)(Raiffa 1982). Figuring out whether there is a ZOPA is much more difficult. It requires putting oneself in the shoes of the numerous other parties, and gathering the information needed to make a multidimensional estimate of the overlap among the likely interests of all the stakeholders.

3.4 Conclusion:

This chapter had shed light over a number of approaches that dealt with trans-boundary water conflicts, we discussed the earlier the importance to differentiate between conflict and dispute, then we moved and discussed the intensity of water conflicts, we had also detailed the role of power in shaping the hydro-politics and hydro-hegemony, then we discussed the water diplomacy approach and the importance of negotiation theory in shaping water conflict and managing them.

The chapter also discussed the dynamics of water international law, we shed light over its strengths and weaknesses, we also went through the rhetoric's of water conflict, walking through the two schools of water conflict

Water conflicts occur when natural, societal, and political domains interact. Together, these interactions generate the dynamics of water, if the interaction was toward solving or escalating water conflicts,

Water diplomacy, is a promising filed in conflict management over trans-boundary conflicts, or in other words International water consensus building. As demography changes and population grows, economic development, and climate change impose pressure on finite water resources (Hanqin 2003), interventions at critical nodes and links of these networks will become increasingly important. Science alone is not sufficient to resolve conflicts within these networks. Nor is policy-making that does not take science into account likely to yield resilient solutions(Heather L. Beach, Jesse Hammer 2000)(Priscoli 1996). Rather, resilient solutions are most likely to be found through a negotiated approach that blends science, policy, and politics to understand and manage complex water problems(Velma I. Grover 2007)(Susskind & Shafiqul Islam 2013).

We need a different approach that takes account of these complexities. In our view, instead of thinking about managing systems that are bounded and made up of components that interact in predictable ways, it is more helpful to think in terms of complex water networks.

The next chapter will examine the empirical case study in the light of the theories discussed in this chapter.

4.0   Chapter Four:
Case Study: The Jordanian -
Israeli Water conflict

4.1 Introduction

The main focus of this chapter is analyzing the Jordanian-Israeli water conflict through analyzing the situation before the Peace Treaty which was signed in year 1994 and the situation in the post treaty. The peace treaty includes Annex II which is also referred as the water agreement and the water issues part. This chapter will start by giving a brief history on the water situation in the Middle East and the challenged among nations whom are sharing trans-boundary water resources.

The chapter will reflect the theories of the previous chapter upon the Jordanian – Israeli water conflict and pin point the challenges and dilemmas facing both parties it will also discuss issues of hydro-politics and the power asymmetries, the chapter will also evaluate the negotiation process of the peace treaty and focusing on water related issues, a brief history of the negotiation process will be mentioned just to acknowledge the reader of my thesis of the long-history of conflict and the attempts to overcome obstacles and their failures.

4.2 Understanding the Jordan-Israeli water issues:

Middle East and North Africa (MENA) region are home to almost (5%)of the world's people, but have less than (1 %) of the world's renewable fresh water(Bard 2007)(World Bank 1996). The problem is most acute among Israel and Jordan. Both states are considered among the 10 most water-scarce countries in the world, Scarcity of water is the largest socio-politic-economo-environmental challenge that faces Jordan and Israel today (Steenhuis,

2010). The conflict over water is a hot topic. Despite existing water agreement, water is considered as a scares resources, increasingly affected by pollution uses, whether for agricultural or industrial uses or even for daily needs (Berman & Wihbey 1999) due to natural growth and regional instability, wars and deteriorating politics and fleeing refugees, causing demographic instability, have emphasized the strategic importance of fresh water among neighboring states. Water is becoming a medium for conflict and peace, water is considered as an issue of national security, it plays a major role is shaping foreign policy as well as domestic strategies. Given water's influential abilities to redefine interstate relations.

Among the many controversial issues in Middle East, water is considered one of them; this sheds light over trans-boundary water issues as a highly politicized topic. Many researches claim that the Arab-Israeli conflict is mainly because of water issues (Benvenisti 2004; Benvenisti & Associa- 2013; Berman & Wihbey 1999; Biswas 1994; Drake 2007; Fisher 2001; Franklin M. Fisher 2010; Giordano et al. 2013; Gleick 1993; Gleick 2013; Haftendorn 2000; Lowi 2003), many other researchers emphasize on other more strategic issues to ignite conflict and eliminating water as the kernel cause, (smuggling weapons by Arab guerrillas to Israel, planning attacks on sensitive places, Haddadin 2002), this can drive us to a conclusion that water could be cause for water conflict but not the main reason.

Whatever might have been the historic or political circumstances that put Jordan and Israel under a very water conflict situation; there is no basis today for our practice of judging the value of Jordan River water to be negligible. All resources, commodities, and services have value. River Jordan is often a valuable resource, whether judged by the direct daily essential use or by its less obvious ecological functions.

The longer we ignore or distort water conflicts, the more overused, degraded, and misallocated the resource becomes. Without a proper allocation mechanism to help guide and tame water conflict and to create a means of cooperation, nothing much can be done to create a resilient situation benefiting all.

4.2.1 Current pressure on water:

The Water conflict in the Middle East presents a serious challenge to policy makers. Can states in the region formulate an integrated policy towards water efficiency? Or will it lead to a humanitarian disaster?

With the "Arab spring phenomena" reaching Syria, a number of refugee started to flee the country to Jordan, Turkey and Lebanon, since most of the Jordanians are relationally interlinked to Syria, among other facilitating things, around 1.2 million refugee reached Jordan, less numbers fled to Turkey and Lebanon, it is estimated that around 3,000 Syrians cross the Jordanian boarders daily (Fedorov 2013), around 30% of the Syrians are kept at refugee camps(Anon 2013), the rest have more social links with Jordanian people and manage to stay with them, this situation had affected the demographic stability of Jordan, as a small country with limited opportunities. The latest unofficial consensus if that Jordan reached 10 million inhabitant with an increase of one million yearly (Haddadin, Nsour, 2014)

During the modern history, Jordan has been always asylum for neighboring countries, it is estimated that around 70% of Jordan population are refugees(UNRWA 2013). "The

82

Syrian refugee emergency is highlighting one of Jordan's most pressing problems — water," says Christian Snoad, Oxfam's water, sanitation and hygiene coordinator in Za'atari,(Baker 2013) in a recently released statement. "Solutions need to be found to deal with Jordan's water scarcity, and this will need to be done as a matter of urgency."

Figure 7: view shows the Zaatari refugee camp (Mafraq-Jordan) on July 18, 2013 (Blair 2013)

Such a volatile situation that erupts almost constantly (Palestinian refugees, Iraq gulf war. etc.) Brings us to how a small country like Jordan with almost no valuable resources could cope politically, economically and socially with these on ground transition.

Among the many resources that are stressed with such situation water is one of them, Water is considered a scarce limited resource. Another major player in water limitations is the precipitation; Water is the key player feature in the (population/resource) calculus, water resources in Jordan and Israel are considered to be limited and the country's population continues to grow. A high rate of natural population growth of over 2.8% (TALOZI 2007), annual growth rate, combined with massive influxes of refugees on the Jordanian side. The situation in Jordan is much harsh than in Israel, most households in Jordan as an example; get once every week for a number of hours to fill their roof mounted cisterns, in many cases the pressure of the water is low to reach the roof cisterns. Jordanian and Israeli water resources are unable to cope with population in a sustainable manner, Its water shortage problem has been exacerbated by the political situations, which has transformed into an imbalance condition between population and water.

What makes the Jordan-Israeli water conflict is an interesting and unique case to study?. That is because of its unique characteristics; first one is its long history of supply-side management while ignoring demand management, secondly because of its Growing pressures on water resources supply, both in terms of quantity and quantity, deriving from regional instability and economic development. And finally due to its incompatibility between hydrogeological and political boundaries due to political conflicts.

4.2.2 The Arab-Israeli water conflict:

The roots of the Arab-Israeli conflict dates back to the late nineteenth century, with the Jewish immigration to Palestine, and the later establishment of the State of Israel in 1948, which triggered armed conflicts that lasted for decades (Shamir and Haddadin, 2003). The roots of conflict over the waters of the Jordan River lies in the convergence of two phenomena, one material, the other historical and ideological. There has been a history of conflict in the region leading, in quite a few cases, to military action in the Jordan River basin The June War of 1967, known as The Six Day War, was a decisive event that altered the nature of the conflict as much it altered the positioning of the co-riparian's and the water allocation and utilization of the river basin. For the Arab countries, the outcome of this war was deemed as a defeat (Lowi 2003), while few other researches as mentioned earlier claim the opposite.

In order to Establishing a point of departures for the whole issue, the story started by considering water as a scarce and finite source, much of Middle Eastern water comes from two major basins: the Jordan river system and the Yarmouk river system. confined reliance on these resources has made water an agitator for conflict, stimulating confrontations such as the 1967 War (fomented by Syria's attempts to divert water from lake Tiberias which was occupied by Israel, ending by occupying the whole Golan heights(Wolf 1995), Recognition of water's role as an obstacle in interstate relations has promoted numerous attempts at resolution, including diplomatic efforts ending with the signing of 1994 Israeli-Jordanian peace Treaty.

4.2.3 The Jordanian-Israeli water conflict:

Jordan River is a trans-boundary river sharing its water among Israel and Jordan, Israel has a full control over the upstream, and the downstream is considered as forming the political borders among the two states, this condition has exacerbated the situation. The situation has been intensified by the fact that Jordan River shares most of its surface water resources with neighboring countries; their control on water has partially disallowed Jordan of its fair share of water. The cooperation between Israel and Jordan, codified through The peace treaty, did not develop much beyond the declaration of a peace treaty, similar to the relationship between the previously signed treaty between Egypt and Israel (Scheumann & Schiffler 1998). Current use of water already exceeds its renewable supply. The deficit is covered by the unsustainable practice of overdrawing aquifers, resulting in lowering water tables and affecting the overall water quality. Conventional water resources cannot cope anymore with the escalating water demands, the deficits are being covered by mining of groundwater beyond the safe yields, and in some cases by over exploiting of nonrenewable groundwater, this raises the question regarding future demands, and the strategy how to augment the gap?.

Water resource in the middle east are reaching a critical stage. Nevertheless The 1994 peace treaty, had established a comprehensive guidelines regulating the allocation of water from the Jordan and Yarmouk Rivers. Conflicts over water has always been a hot topic between the two countries. Jordan, depend on the underground non-renewable water aquifer sources and to some extend on Jordan River, has experienced an enormous escalating water shortage due to the climatically and political instability in the region. At the same time, Israel on the other hand is utilizing all available water from its National

Water System[5] has been forced to resort to overexploitation of available resources for expanding agricultural and industrial ventures (Sherman 1993).

Water has become a one of the major conflict agitator between Jordan and Israel, the conflict has escalated by the regions dry climate and lack of precipitation. Facing a growing deficit in fresh water supplies brought about by lingering drought conditions, Israel halved Jordan's annual allocation of 50 MCM of water in March 1999. Jordan was hit hard, and found itself unable to cope with current levels of consumption, declaring drought conditions and mandating water rationing in May 1999 (Berman & Wihbey 1999).

4.2.4   The Jordanian-Israeli water needs:

The total amount of annual renewable ground water resources underlying the territories of Israel, Jordan, has been estimated at 2900 MCM with varying water quality, the total withdrawal of ground water accounted for about 3100 MCM, about 1900 MCM by Israel, and about 1200 MCM by Jordan (Hussein 2002), The balance shows an overdraft of about 200 MCM, Such mining of non-renewable ground water stocks leads to dropping ground water tables and, depending on the circumstances, might result in the intrusion of deep saline water, negatively affecting the quality of the water. An overview of the current regional water allocation is indicated in (Table 4).

---

[5] consisting of the West Bank Mountain Aquifer, the Coastal Aquifer and the Lake Tiberias Basin.

Country	Annual renewable resource	Annual withdrawals	Annual withdrawals (%)	Per capita Liter/day	Water usage (%)Domestic	Water usage (%)Industry	Water usage (%)Agriculture
Jordan	800	1,200	125	147	20	5	75
Israel	2,100	1,900	90	375	16	5	79

Table 13 Water Resources; Pacific Institute for Studies in Development, Environment and Security, Stockholm Environment Institute, and World Bank Estimates(Hussein 2002)

The largest water consumer in the region is agriculture, maintains a relatively high absolute level of water use. Agricultural water supply is significantly subsidized in Israel and Jordan. In Israel in recent decades efforts have been made to increase the productive (or technical) water efficiency of the agricultural sector through fixed allocations and the introduction of modern water-saving irrigation technologies (Scheumann & Schiffler 1998). However, irrigation water tariffs are subsidized and the absolute level of use is still high compared with the total regional water availability, beside agriculture contribution to the GDP is 6% in 2010, and about 6% of the labor force is employed in agriculture. (Alkhaddar et al. 2005). The regional conflict on water rights is a conflict over the control of water resources and their allocation. it is neither a conflict about the allocation of a 'free good', since conventional water resources have a cost, nor about the allocation of an absolutely limited good, since further fresh water production is at least theoretically possible through several technological devices such as seawater desalination or water imports. The distributional conflict on water is superimposed by the political and ideological components: water as a symbol of sovereignty and water as an instrument for other political goals.(Zeitoun 2008)(Scheumann & Schiffler 1998).

4.3   The peace negotiation process:

This chapter aims to shed light over the peace process journey that was incarnated in the signing of a peace treaty among Jordan and Israel, this chapter will discuss shortly the pre-treaty process and the post treaty implementations, it will also discuss the peace treaty and the water Annex II issues "water agreement"

4.7.1   Background:

The architecture of the peace process evolved after the Madrid Conference in October 1991, but before the 1994 peace treaty a long history of water negation's is revealed, the process dates back to 1920 when France and Great Britain signed several treaties on the behalf of their colonizes, a second treaty was signed in 1926 between once again France and great Britain over the Yarmouk river.

Date	Treaty Basin	Signatories	Name
Sep-28/1995	River Jordan	Israel, Palestine (PLO)	Israeli-Palestinian interim agreement on the west bank and Gaza annex I
Oct-26/1994	Araba groundwater, Yarmouk river,	Israel - Jordan	Peace Treaty

	Jordan river		
Dec-31/1955	Jordan River	Israel Jordan, Lebanon, Syria	Johnston Negotiations
Feb-2/1926	Jordan	Great Britain and France	Agreement on good neighborly relations between GB and France
Dec-23/1920	Jordan, Tigris-Euphrates, Yarmouk river	Great Britain and France	Exchange of notes constituting an agreement between GB and France, respecting boundary line between Syria and Palestine

Table 14: Previous water treaties (Wolf et al. 2003)

In early 1950s Israeli government made its plans public by embarking on draining Huleh Lake, at the northern parts of Jordan river and constructing a national water carrier that will reach the lowest land in the south of Negev Desert (Wolf 1996), in year 1951 Jordan announced its plans to irrigate the lower lands of Jordan rift valley known as Ghour (lower lands in Arabic) at the same time Israeli closed the dam at the lower part of the Sea of Galilee preventing Jordan and Syria from water, These actions led to a series of border skirmishes between Israel and Syria, Syria had opened fire on construction workers, this situation created a tense ground, in year 1953 President Eisenhower sent his special envoy, Eric Johnston, in an attempt to mediate a comprehensive complex situation, Johnston based on a study prepared by Tennessee Valley Authority prepared a water allocation scheme to be deployed by Jordan, Syria and Israel, the proposal also known as the Unified plan allocated 400 MCM per year to

Israel, 720 MCM per year to Jordan, 35 MCM per year to Lebanon, and 132 MCM per year to Syria, The technical committees from both sides accepted the Unified Plan but momentum died in the political realm, and the Plan was never ratified.

Dr. Haddadin in his book (Haddadin 2002) documents that Johnston plan was the bench mark for the 1994 peace treaty negotiation in an attempt to reach the numbers allocated in the "Unified Plan", many researches who examined and compared between both the Unified plan and the peace treaty water annex showed that if unified plan was the base then the Jordanian negotiators did very bad (Abukhater 2010).

As Wolf et al. (2003) indicates in Table 14 that Throughout history, several water schemes were prepared to put in place the waters of the Jordan River both Arabs and Israelis unilaterally proposed many plans to govern and manage the utilization of the rivers, unfortunately These plans, as they provided national solutions to a regional problem, failed to address the overall regional dimension of water and caused further tension and stressful situation, this falls under main reason that During these years there was no real direct channels of communication (Selby 2005)(Haddadin 2002).

Water cooperation between Jordan and Israel faced many challenges, one of the critical issues, Jordanian uses the water from river Jordan to irrigate agriculture that is grown in the areas adjacent to the river, while Israel had diverted huge amounts of water from the River Jordan to areas far away from the original basin, the second issue is the lack of an international body to overlook and monitor the use of water on both sides, this drives both side to the prisoners dilemma, were each part starts to enlarge their share of the pie, the state that controls the upstream has an overall monopoly. Syrian and Jordanian parties agreed on incorporating Litani River into the River Jordan water systems, this issue while it attempts to enlarge the amount of water available in the River Jordan system had excerpted the situation, as there is a large amount of the water going to Israel, Syria claimed that Israel should not have access to one drop of the River Jordan water. The final issue is the game of numbers, the qualitative allocation of water amounts, the needs are manipulated by numbers, by defining the "water quota" for each state; this issue creates another dimension to the problem.

On October 26, 1994, the State of Israel and Jordan signed a Peace Treaty that included a water agreement the treaty distinguishes bilateral and multilateral negotiation tracks. In the bilateral, Israel separately negotiates with the Palestine Liberation Organization (PLO), Palestinian Authority, Jordan and Syria all major political issues at stake. In the multilaterals, five separate working groups on specific topics have been established, with representatives of the region and other interested countries and international organization's addressing water, environment, economic relations, refugees and arms control.

Within the course of negotiation priorities were divided into two categories, high level priorities and low level priorities, high level priorities included security, mutual recognition, land, and borders, low level priorities included issues related to water, natural resources, refugees, environment and regional development, what may be concluded that in many cases solving the low level priorities such as water issues facilitated solving high level priorities politics (Priscoli & Wolf 2008).

In the Bilateral negotiations according to Annex II[6], Israel and Jordan aim to gain additional water for River Jordan through better management of parts of the Jordan's catchment areas, including the ability to store water in Lake Tiberias during winter season, and supplying River Jordan with necessary amount when needed, it's also included options for utilizing Yarmouk River and through the mobilization of other resources.

The negotiation process was a bumpy unpaved road to walk, it went through several ups and downs, the team during the negotiation process followed several steps. The first was the identification of the major critical problems, substantively address future water issues and searching for possible solutions. The main aim of the five multilateral groups; was to establish a concrete foundation for the later and reinforce peace. Dr. Haddadin (Head of Jordanian water negotiators), claimed that: "the sequence is restoration, mitigation, and cooperation, meaning restoration of rights, mitigation of adverse impacts resulting from the creation of Israel, and then cooperation would start" (Haddadin 2002)

Although the two bilateral and multilateral tracks of negotiations were meant to complement one another, clashes occurred and more coordination between the two arenas was needed on certain issues (Shamir and Haddadin, 2003).

It is highly important to walk the reader of my thesis through the peace treaty process (conflict resolution life cycle, as explained is chapter 3) even shortly just to address the three stages of a conflict resolution the first stage is the

---

[6] The Jordanian – Israeli Peace treaty 1994 Annex II of the Treaty is related to Water Related Matters

pre-negotiation the second stage is the official negotiation process ending in signing the agreement, the final stage or the implementation stage.

4.7.2 The pre-negotiation:

The main purpose of these of the pre-negotiations process is to facilitate dialogs among participants. this joint fact finding process helps in providing a form of conciliation and precisely identifying major issues, interests, needs, and concerns of both parties, which were consensually outlined and made clear to everyone. These pre-negotiation efforts helped in meeting the "other" party, understanding how history is politically manipulated, and examining potential cooperation.

There have been a number of pre-negotiation rounds prior to the official negotiation process that embarked in the 1990s which was a natural evolution of the 1994 Peace Treaty. During this stage, all affected parties (stakeholders) must be identified and included in the process to avoid the ex parte adverse impacts that might arise by excluding important stakeholders. It was clear that this treaty had ignored or even refused in many cases to include all parties, the main focus was on the Jordanian Israeli side ignoring many sharing parties as Lebanon and Syria, making separate bilateral negotiation with each party alone had complicated the scene. It was clearly an Israeli strategy to maximize their gains which affected many parties to withdraw from the peace talks (Haddadin 2002).

Another important step is to identify the aspiration base for all parties, or what are the gains attempted to be reached by each party, this could be reached by each party indulges in a joint fact finding process, most of the talks during this stage were technical driven talks, the main focus was on hydrological technical aspects. These meeting had paved the road for the 1994 Treaty, and building trust among negotiators (Haddadin & Uri Shamir 2003). Many researchers argue that these pre-negotiation meeting were necessary to establish trust and confidence building measures (CBMs)[7] and in creating a conductive mutually trusted atmosphere.

Other researcher's argue (Abukhater 2013)(Mostafa Faraj 2014) that the pre-negotiation process failed in establishing the long-term trust and confidence that was intended in first place, due to the ongoing accusations of both parties of the misuse or over-exploitation and hegemony of water resources. Another goal of pre-negotiation meetings was to establish a data bank for all related issues, each party started to stretch and deliberately to overestimate the number as a strategy to enlarge their pie of Winnings, the other side of the problem is that neither the Israelis nor the Jordanians questioned the validity of the water related data (Trolldalen 1997). This on the other hand, affected the long-term trust worthy intended relationship. The problem was mixing political driven problems with technical data, According to the Israeli Ministry of Foreign Affairs, 1995, these bilateral talks continued for almost two years in Washington and resulted in the signing of the Israeli-Jordanian Common Agenda on September 14, 1993 (Abukhater 2010).

---

[7] Confidence Building Measures (CBMs) are broadly defined as measures that address, prevent, or resolve uncertainties among states. Designed to prevent wanted and especially unwanted escalations of hostilities and build mutual trust, CBMs can be formal or informal, unilateral, bilateral, or multilateral, military or political, and can be state-to-state or non-governmental (http://csis.org/programs/international-security-program/asia-division/cross-strait-security-initiative-/confidence-b)

4.7.3 The Negotiation Process:

   The Peace treaty negotiations were political in nature, scope, and focus, it took the form of bilateral talking's with no third party or mediator involvement's except in a number cases were USA and Russia had pushed both parties to overcome obstacles by offering informal advices, the first round took place in *The Madrid Conference,* the impact of power imbalance was neutralized to lead a fair and constructive negotiation. The Israeli side was keen on naturalizing their relationships with Arabs. Arabs on the other hand were very skeptical, the USA and Russia played the role of the sponsors of the peace process. The second round was called *Washington D.C. bilateral talks,* what signifies these talks is they were of a secret nature and kept out of public, this position had roared the public at both states to consider that definitely the outcome is less than expected and less fair. The Third round of talks, took place at the Dead Sea they were called The *Middle East bilateral talks,* The negotiations took a more substantive and serious turn as they moved to the Middle East (Haddadin 2002; Haddadin & Uri Shamir 2003), at this moment USA stepped in and made the Washington declaration, the friendly relationships between the leaders of both countries had smoothen the process, the declaration affirmed that the agreement between Jordan and Israel will never deprive other trans-boundary nations from their rights to water, this declaration made it easier for negotiators as they shifted focusing towards interest and not gains, at this moment parties started to negotiate and to look beyond the limits of the problem, they discussed the possibility of co-operation around several projects such as the Red-Sea-Dead-Sea water channel. During the last round of the painful negotiations held at Eilat and Aqaba the goal was to reach a comprehensive peace treaty and to deescalate undesired hostility.

Challenges to negotiation: both negotiators were faced with a number of complexity issues: The Palestinian rights to water, Jordan negotiated as the amount allocated for Palestine should be considered as a Jordan west bank side, later by the advice of late King Hussein, Jordan has exempted the Palestinian share as the Palestinian side will negotiate for themselves (Haddadin 2002). The Jordanian side tried to push a previously signed agreement between Jordan and Israel regarding water as discussed earlier the (Johnston) Plan, appeared to be problematic for Jordan. Reducing the current Israeli use of the Yarmouk River from 75 MCM to 25 MCM (Haddadin 2002), and the second is the uncertainty of the amount of water in Yarmouk river, as the Syrian are already utilizing the same riparian. Jordan also insisted applying international law, while the Israeli side tried to deny the applicability of the international law by claiming that the International law does not provide a template for conflict resolution. This sheds light upon the importance of involving all stakeholders in the negotiation process, both parties the Jordanian and Israeli failed to collaboratively acknowledge the issue of the Syrian water allocation in a rational manner.

4.7.4   Israel-Jordan Treaty of Peace, 1994

On October 26, 1994, Israel and Jordan signed a Peace Treaty at Wadi Arava/Araba, this treaty included an annex II which is also referred to as the water agreement, the main intend of the treaty was to end a long years of conflict and struggle, and to achieve a sustainable long lasting peace, through developing and maintaining mutual cooperation, and ensuring national security and sovereignty. Annex II attempts to put forth an allocation scheme to resolve the shared international waters in dispute, Annex II provides general principles and guidance for a comprehensive and lasting settlement over water allocation, regarding water as a basis for advancing cooperation between the two countries. Annex II of the Treaty outlines details about the target source/location of water transfer, the amounts of water transferred for each party, quality, times of the year, and the financial arrangement.

4.7.5   Treaty Implementation:

This stage included the implementation and monitoring and reassessing of the treaty, by developing a monitoring mechanism to overview and examine the follow-up of the agreement, during the period 1994-1996 after the signing of the water treaty, the region was under a severe draught, that affected the whole treaty as Israel deprived Jordan from its share, claiming that the water amount are insufficient for its national needs, the defects of the treaty had been unraveled by issue of uncertainty and contradictory interpretations. On the other hand, 50% of the Yarmouk River was transferred to Amman city (EXACT, 2005), water supply was intermittent to twice a week (Biswas & Bino, 2001).

Apparently the implementation of the Treaty seems problematic, slow, and difficult. Summer is always a glorious moment to melt treaties and expose them. In year 1999 Jordan received 50MCM of water, which accounts to third of the amount agreed by the treaty, and accounts for 10% of its annual demand, that was a caused by the climatic change and the drought that hit the area for two continuous years, Israel was unable to deliver the amount agreed upon in the treaty from lake Tiberias (Innes and Booher, 1999). This incident draw upon the defects of the treaty as there was no mention to a drought management clauses (Haddadin & Uri Shamir 2003), the table 6 below shows the treaty water allocated for each party in MCM

Water allocations in the Israel-Jordan Peace Treaty (MCM)		
Jordan	Israel	Implications
- Yarmouk River residual for Jordan (estimated between 60-282 MCM)	- Jordan River residual for Israel (estimated at 600 MCM)	- Undetermined and varied amounts - Greater uncertainty for Jordan as a result of the unregulated Syrian use of the Yarmouk - Israel maintained its current use of the Jordan River
- 20 from Jordan River (summer)	20 from Yarmouk (winter)	- Israel utilizes Lake Tiberias for storage of floodwater - Jordan has no storage facilities
-10 from desalinated water in north	- Maintaining existing use in Araba +	- Israel's existing use given higher priority

	Additional10 from Araba groundwater in south	
- 50 "additional water"	- 25 from Yarmouk (12 summer, 13 winter)	- Guaranteed amounts for Israel - Uncertain and unguaranteed 50 additional water for Jordan - Ambiguous cost sharing (Jordan will cover cost)
Total (before treaty): 120-130 Total (after treaty): 90-312	Total (before treaty): 640-690 Total (after treaty): 625-665	- Overall Israel is allocated more water - Israel maintained its current volumetric water

Table 15 : Louka, 2006; Sosland, 2007; Elmusa, 1995

The comparison among the two water allocation treaties (table #) shows clearly the Jordan gains are much less than the gains of the unified plan, this clearly refutes the argument made by Dr. Haddadin that Jordan in the 1994 peace treaty, gained not only all the allocated amount discussed in the unified plan but much more.

	Negotiations Outcome (1994)	Unified Plan (1955)
Yarmouk River	- Israel receives 20 MCM in winter - Israel receives 12 MCM in summer and 13 MCM in winter (total of 25 MCM), and Jordan receives the residual of	Israel receives 25MCM and Jordan receives 377 from the Yarmouk.

	the flow (estimated between 60-282 MCM). - Undetermined and varied amounts for Jordan - Greater uncertainty for Jordan as a result of the unregulated Syrian use of the Yarmouk	
Jordan River	- Israel receives residual of the Jordan River (estimated at 600 MCM) - Israel maintained its current use of the Jordan River	Israel receives 375 from the Jordan, Jordan receives 100 from the Jordan

Table 16: a comparison between the peace treaty 1994 and the unified plan of 1955 **(Abukhater 2010)**

4.4 Analyzing the Jordan Israeli water conflict:

This part will reflect the methodology and frameworks developed in chapter 3 over the case study, it will analyze the water conflict intensity, water and power, water international law, water diplomacy and negotiation and its applications over the Jordan Israeli water conflict.

4.4.1 Water Conflict intensity:

Both Jordan and Israel have a chronic water shortage problem. Due to many reason the major one is low amount of precipitations (Pamukcu 2003). This problem imposes an increasing burden upon the state administration and the policy makers, and calls for intelligent and economic solutions and prudent water management. Israel remain river basin hegemons and regional superpowers, Israel had put its power in all dimensions to use to determine varying intensities of dominative forms of hydro-hegemony. Israel controls 90% of the shared surface and groundwater resources (Zeitoun & Elisa 2010).

The situation along the Jordan River is more extreme. It has cursorily been shown that Israel has achieved a negative/dominative form of hydro-hegemony through strategies of resource capture (with capture of territory in 1967) and containment (through the signing of treaties skewed in the hegemon's favor with Jordan and the Palestinians, as well as by coercion-pressure, securitization and military force employed to contain co-riparian's Syria and Lebanon). One way that Israel maintains the consolidated control it has over the water resources is through the use of institutional structure which is called the Joint Water Committee (JWC). Selby (Selby 2007) has described the Joint Water Committee as a tool more of domination than of cooperation

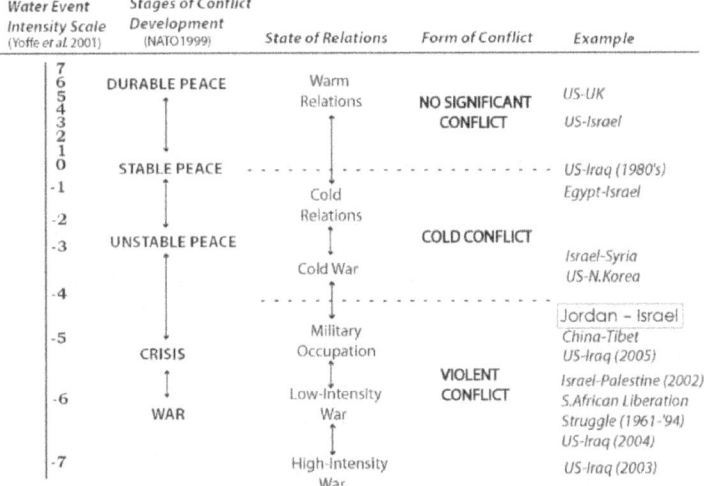

Figure 8: Conflict Intensity Frame. (Zeitoun & Elisa 2010) modified by Author

Water shortage, accompanied by high population growth and successive periods of drought, is becoming an increasing cause of stress and is likely to have a significant impact on the future political and economical framework of the Middle East (Steenhuis, 2010:141). Water Problem is growing day by day in both number and intensity, that is related to the critical role water plays in a such sensitive area. Unless both parties address the seriousness of the situation and shift from competing each other into a more collaborative approach both will suffer.

4.7.1 Water and power:

This part will demonstrated the merit in viewing trans-boundary contexts through a lens of critical hydro-politics. This part focus has been on the role of power and power asymmetry in the purely political question of 'who gets how much water, when, where and why?

Water is the major geopolitical factor in Middle East (Trolldalen 1997); it is one of the main driving forces for the peace process and stability in the region. The strategic challenge for the future is to ensure adequate quantity and quality of water to meet human and ecological needs in the face of growing competition among domestic, industrial–commercial, agricultural, and environmental uses specially in a region were uncertainty is the only certain issue, decision makers at all levels of government will need to make informed choices among often conflicting and uncertain alternative actions. These choices are best made with the full benefit of research and analysis.

Jordan more than Israel is facing a future of very stressful water resources (among the most stressful in the world on a per capita basis). Available water resources are projected to decline from around 140 cubic meters per capita per year for all uses in 2008 to only 90 cubic meters per capita per year by 2025, putting Jordan in the category of a critical water situation. Unless there are fundamental changes in the way water resources are managed and used, the region as a whole will experience a worsening crisis of water scarcity and economic decline. A vicious circle will set in whereby harsh water shortages adversely affect economic growth, and slower growth in turn constrains the investment needed to improve water availability. This downward spiral would spell disaster for the region(Bard 2007). The situation in Jordan is exacerbated by pollution and by the disproportionate use of water for low-value agriculture, water is a hinder to the whole peace process as A Jerusalem Post headline concisely stated the security threat, "The hand that controls the faucet rules the country." (Jerusalem Post July 16 1996)

The figure below prepared by Zeitoun and Elisa (2010) interpret this visually, the length of the columns were suggesting that the most powerful state may create and maintain a situation of hydro-politics through the development of 'pillars' that support it, The lengths of pillars are relative to other basin states, and not quantified, These plots are based on the current hydro-political context.

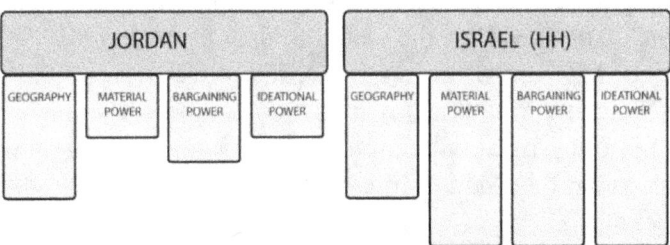

Figure 9: Suggested plots of hydro-hegemonic configurations (Zeitoun & Elisa 2010)
Hydro-hegemony presents a real challenge to the status quo of hydro-politics.

4.7.2   Water Diplomacy:

Water policy in the Middle East and specially in the case of the Jordanian Israeli water conflict has been subject to significant pressure from environmental and political forces. Water diplomacy appears to provide an example of the difficulties of managing a trans-boundary water issues. The evolution of Israel's water diplomacy indicates that its policy-makers - having understood the limitations of their arid environment - are looking alternative waters, which means enlarging the water pie, both to the sea and to the region's wetter lands to generate more water instead of coming to accept the need to live within their hydrological means. Arnon Soffer, the water advisor at the Israeli Foreign Ministry offers a more realistic view (Dolatyar 2002), saying that "the day must soon come when the Israeli policy-makers begin to allocate water according to economic rather than political priorities"

The case of Jordan and Israel shows how even countries at war can negotiate a water agreement if it is framed in non-zero-sum terms and trust continues to be built over time. The problem lies in the carrying on of the agreements as well the agreement itself, nevertheless parties reached agreement as the upper political will of the leaders of both countries pushed the negotiations, still water conflict are not fully solved or managed. The water diplomacy theory provides a window of opportunity, the question remains is it applicable in real world?. It becomes clear that water diplomacy works in multilateral agreements when all trans-boundary stakeholders are involved, but it falls short in the unilateral agreements

4.5 Conclusion:

Water is considered as a two way sword, a driver of conflict as well as peace, the allocation of shared water resources, land division and international border, normalization and achieving viable and sustainable peace in the region are key issues that the two countries need to address through negotiation. By highlighting critical details about the root causes and nature of the conflict

Criteria	Indicators	Result
History of Water wars	The reality of water wars in history Water as a cause of war Water influence war	No Yes
Conflict Theory	Conflict or dispute? Cause–effect relationships Systems and sub-systems are clearly bounded Easily predict the future.	Conflict - - - -
Conflict intensity	Bar -7/+7 Conflict intensity Cause and effect linkages are likely to be unclear	-4 High +
Water and power	Power = Hydro-stability or Power = Hydro-hegemony Political factors	Hydro-hegemony ++
Water international law	Willing to apply international law Emphasizing international law The ability to force	- + - +

	applying international law	-
		+
	Accountability	
	Third Party involvement	
	arbitration	
Negotiation Theory	Bilateral	+
	Multilateral	-
	overcome deadlock	-
	Agreement among relevant stakeholders on means and ends is not hard to establish	-
	Joint problem-solving	+
	Bargaining or negotiation	
	Holding on BATNA	-
	Steering the network towards an agreed-upon future state	- -
	Fair allocation	
	Uncertainty addressed	
Water Diplomacy	Joint fact finding	0/+
	Mutual Gains	-
	significant sensitivity	-
	New modes of operating and managing are likely to be required.	-
	water professionals are deeply cognizant of the network's initial configurations	+
	Causes may not be proportional to effects, non-linear feedback	-
		0
	Move toward the best possible solution space.	-

Table 17: Summary of the criteria adopted in the case study analysis

Did the agreement achieved the moving the situation from hydro-hostility towards hydro-stability?. The previous mentioning of the peace treaty and the analysis of the water agreement "Annex-II" of the agreement had many deficits such as the agreement does not seem to consider the adverse consequences of Israel's previous and current water development on Jordan, the agreement ignored the international law and considered it as impractical , and urged for a more pragmatic solution to bridge the gap of communication as the Israeli claimed by Dr. Shamir (Haddadin & Uri Shamir 2003). The treaty stated that Jordan receives its water just after Israel takes its required share made Jordan stand as a Risk Taker. On the whole, the Treaty is vague with regard to parties this left the treaty with destructive ambiguity (Itay Fischhendler 2008) instead of being constructive ambiguity, which threats the treaty implementation and the overall durability and sustainability. Nevertheless water and security are closely intertwined. The agreement managed to establish channels of diplomacy, peace, and cooperation and putting an end to a long period of hostility and conflict are the mutual gains for both Israel and Jordan.

During the negotiations boarders arms and security were the hot topics, they were never blown out of their frame, water was negotiated only on technical terms and amounts and never on a more strategic level.

Another major point of the treaty, is its ignorance for environmental issues, there was no mentioning of the depleted environmental effects on lake Tiberius cause by Israeli over usage of water through their national carrier, any agreement that don't take the sustainable allocation of environmental issues will have a serious consequences that may harm the integrity of the environment. And another corner stone issues, the treaty does not mention the rights of future generation in using fresh water resources.

The formal negotiations were merely dominated by politically-charged matters, or issues of "high" politics, such as security, mutual recognition, land, borders, refugee, and Jerusalem. Water was negotiated only on the technical level. Apparently water was considered as a sub-level problem issues, it is clearer by analyzing the Jordanian Israeli case that water can never be a cause of war, it could be one of the reason leading but not the driving one.

Main points:
- Focusing on bilateral treaties instead of multilateral peace treaty,
- Multilateral agreements are much harder to attain but once reached they create a much more stable situation and a more resilient and robust conditions
- Bilateral agreements are easier to obtain but the may exclude several parties that are considered as influential stakeholders, which could undermine the whole treaty
- It was conceived that low political issues once solved will pave the road for the higher political issues, this argument has been prove to lack insight, unless higher political issues are solved lower political issues will remain just thoughts on paper, cooperation and collaboration among low issues such as water can't be attained without the permission of the higher political issues
- Considering water among the low priorities politics proves that water can't be regarded as the main cause of any future conflict that may escalate into a regional war.

Some other general notes::

- The sudden erupted unrest and wars in neighboring countries, causing a huge amount of people to seek refuge in Jordan, causing more pressure on water resources.
- The risks that both sides must face were never addressed, while Jordan's risks are purely societal psychology, whereas Israel's barriers are largely technical. (Farooq Mitha 2010)

5. Chapter Five:
Findings and conclusions

5.1 Introduction:

In this final chapter, outcomes from all research steps discussed in previous chapters will be brought together in order to answer the central research question and draw well-founded and clear conclusions. This chapter will be providing concluding findings related to the case study, and general conclusion, the chapter will also provide lessons learnt from the examination and the analysis of the research conducted.

Where history has conspired to bring nations to conflict, nature has deprived the inhabitants of the most vital of all resources – water, Nations and their politics have further conspired to hinder the achievement of any cooperative solutions to the water conflicts. Nevertheless populations continue to grow to the point that people can no longer afford the proclivities of conflict.

5.2 Reflecting on the research questions

Derived from the methodology framework discussed in chapter three, and applying the methodology over the Jordanian Israeli water conflict. Going back to the cardinal research question; **What are the characteristics of the Jordanian Israeli water conflict?.** Bearing in mind the long span of the water conflict which dates back to the establishment of State of Israel (1948), water conflict had born. The complexity of adapting a single theory narrows the vision into a reductionist way of analyzing adapting several theories and perspectives enriches the understating of the case, each theory provide us with a part/facet of the answer, nevertheless there is no single theory that claims to hold the only explanation.

Criteria	Findings
History of Water wars	• The case showed that no matter how intense the conflict over trans-boundary waters was it never reached a violent turning point, this case definitely confirms that was over water is hard to be true • The long history of the Israeli Jordanian conflict affirms that peace is the out likely outcome of conflict
Conflict Theory	• The case revealed that the Jordan-Israeli water conflict has a long history dates bake to the 1948 • Causes and effects of water conflict change over time and are dynamic. • The case revealed the difficulty to draw clear boundary over trans-boundary waters, as goes for water allocation schemes • Jordan Israeli water conflict is hard to determine over the future, as future always comes with its uncertainties and surprises .
Conflict intensity	• Jordanian Israeli water conflict was measured to be in the conflict zone of -4, which means it's still far from being a cause of war, the Bar scale also showed that no conflict over

	trans-boundary waters was giving the intensity of -7 (War Zone) • The BAR tool is a very helpful in determining future escalation of de-escalations of conflict, nevertheless the tool is hard to identify causes and effects in predicting future
Water and power	• It was clear that Israel possessed more power and international support than Jordan, beside Israel had a better data and a full control over the lake Tiberius, this position allowed Israel to practice Hydro-hegemony over all co-riparian states including Jordan, this was showed in the draught period after signing the Peace Treaty, when Israel lowered Jordan shares of water, another issue was also when the Jordan river waters were polluted by Israeli plants. At this incident Jordan government tried to cover Israeli breach of the treaty by claiming that the change is smell, color and taste of the water was due to the high temperature season, on the other hand the Israeli tend to embarrass the Jordanian officials by admitting that waters were polluted, creating a huge rage among Jordan citizens against

	their government, this is a clear evidence of hydro-hegemony (Mustafa Faraj 2014)
Water international law	• There is always no willingness from the parties with greater power to opt international law, as international law will deprive them from getting a bigger share, this was clear by the Israeli side as they claimed the inapplicability of international law in such a situation. • Weaker parties always lack the ability to emphasizing international law, and leave it to the third party mediator or the willingness of the other party to apply, in the case of Jordan and Israel, Jordan asked to emphasize on international Law while the Israel, and USA agreed on reaching a solution that may be much relevant as they claimed to the conflict, this tactic by the mediator and Israel reflects that the third party is not totally neutral, it was casted over the Jordanian negotiators are being two against one, so they agreed that anything gained is good at the moment • Third Party involvement arbitration (USA) seems to be uninterested in forcing the implementation of resolutions

Negotiation Theory	• The bilateral negotiations among Jordan and Israel over the River Jordan eliminated several co-riparian states from negotiating their shares and rights to the river, this issue made the agreement vulnerable to uncertainties and never cultivated the full expected outcomes. • The Peace Treaty ignored important stakeholders: the treaty was signed between Jordan and Israel ignoring Syria, while Syria plays a major role as a contributor and a main stakeholder of the Yarmouk River • Holding on BATNA could be a risky issue, especially when there are some power imbalances among states, Jordan needed a resolution, this made Jordan to lower its BATNA, and agree with whatever was offered, in reality Jordan BATNA was it WATNA "Worst alternative to a negotiated agreement" this was clear in the numbers agreed on in the treaty Annex II (See table …) • Lack of transparency and public participation in water conflict resolution will ignite the public against any treaty and lower the chances of cooperation. This

was clear as public on both sides rejected the outcome, and the trickle-down effect of the peace process was never reached

- Addressing uncertainty in agreements is highly important for the sustaining of a long-term treaty, this was never addressed in the Jordan Israeli water agreement, the drought of the summer 1996 had revealed the weaknesses of the treaty
- Ambiguity of the language used in treaties is considered a big hindrance in the implementation, many items in the Jordan Israeli treaty were vague and unclear which left space for interpreting and disagreement among parties.
- All Arab Israeli conflict has never been resolved without the sponsorship of a third party, usually the United States

Water Diplomacy	• joint fact finding was ignored from the Jordanian part, as the day of preparation of the treaty Haddadin, had prepared the agreement without referencing any water allocation to the previously prepared documents, nevertheless Haddadin was forced to do so by the will of upper politics to reach an agreement, this incident reflects two issues, firstly that Jordan was the weaker party and needed

to reach any agreement, preparing a lower BATNA (Haddadin 2002), secondly a disconnectedness among the Experts and the decision makers created a chaotic unclear agreement.

- Mutual Gains approach discusses the interest of both parties and moves beyond the position of each party, water was always on the lower political ladder during the bargaining negotiation, leaving many issues vague and unclear, this affected the mutual gains approach and weakened it.
- Significant sensitivity, many other issues as the Jerusalem and Borders were more sensitive issues than water, but nevertheless water was always played as a pressing card, and interlinked issue affecting the whole package of negotiation.
- The water agreement was a kind of hard bargaining rather than a fair negotiation and water allocation.
- Water professionals were marginalized during the finalization of the water agreement.

Table 18: summary of the research first question

As have been shown earlier in the upper table, each theory is unique in itself, there is no one theory that may provide a comprehensive explanation, this situation could be regarded and in relation to the complexity of the issues over the long span of time that such conflict took place, several changes occurred and the conflict kept moving and changing, the instability of the conflict issues are a clear explanation of the dynamism of conflict, there no single approach or theory that would provide a thorough and absolute explanation.

5.3 Lessons learnt:

Reflecting on the second question of the research; **What are the lessons that can be learned?.** While the knowledge presented in this thesis is context-specific, Neither water cooperation nor conflict is certain in any situation, nevertheless there are still some general lessons that may be learnt and expanded to other trans-boundary water conflicts. Acknowledging these lessons policymakers may increase the likelihood for achieving their policy objectives and managing trans-boundary conflicts:

Criteria	Lessons
History of Water wars	• Water is likely to be one of the reason to ignite and escalate the conflict but could never be a casus belli of war
Conflict Theory	• Water had a value beyond its natural resource value, it was molded in a more controversial meaning, trans-boundary waters are an expression of the sovereignty of the state, each state claimed its historical rights to the waters

	• Water is still used as a pressing component in a packaged conflictual issues,
	• Water conflicts are of a game theory nature, were strategic approach can be sensed among conflictual parties
Conflict intensity	• The Bar scale in a useful tool to identify the intensity of the conflict,
	• It's difficult to link causes and effects while measuring them on the BAR scale to identify future conflict intensity.
Water and power	• Not all power is equal : The better a state's ''hydro hegemony'' position is, the less interest it has in reaching a water conflict resolution, thus a strong third-party involvement will be necessary for successful negotiations
	• The link between water resources and political alternatives is inextricable, with water scarcity leading directly both to increase political tensions to opportunities for cooperation.
	• Political Factors plays a big role and affects water resources as they are considered an indication of state sovereignty
	• Power shapes the willingness and the ability of each states to

	reach and stable statues or to practicing hegemony over water basins
Water international law	• There is always no willingness from the parties with greater power to opt international law, as international law will deprive them from getting a bigger share. • Weaker parties always lack the ability to emphasizing international law, and leave it to the third party mediator or the willingness of the other party to apply, • The ability to force applying international law may prevent some parties from continuing negotiation, it could also emphasize their adaptation to the use game theory "prisoners dilemma " which affects the whole process and weakens the trust bridges built. • The mediator or third party should hold parties accountable to the agreements, the failure to monitor the implementation means a early death certificate to the whole agreement • Third Party involvement arbitration, if any party breach the signed agreement the third party should facilitate and provide documents to the international arbitration

	authority
Negotiation Theory	• The bilateral negotiations unless addressing all trans-boundary riparian's will cause a continuous flow of disagreement among other co-riparian's and prevent the full ripe of the agreement • Ambiguity in the language treaties are shaped will cause future dilemmas and will hinder water agreements and future implementation (I. Fischhendler 2008b) • There should be no Miscommunication between policy makers and the technical parties. • While multilateral agreements seemed very hard, especially when many states refused to negotiate at all, this decision made some states to take further steps and negotiate for themselves in ignorance of the others • As seemed bilateral negotiations are easier to conduct, multi-lateral negotiations holds a the real conflict resolution or management scheme, unless all parties are talking to each other a durable and a long term agreement will be waiting the winds of uncertainty to blow the whole process, to ensure a

sustainable treaty outcome.

- Agreement among relevant stakeholders on means and ends is not hard to establish
- Holding on BATNA could be a risky issue, especially when there are some power imbalances among states,
- Lack of transparency and public participation in water conflict resolution will ignite the public against any treaty and lower the chances of cooperation. This was clear as public on both sides rejected the outcome, and the trickle-down effect of the peace process was never reached
- Uncertainty addressed, unless all issues are addressed specially externalities, any agreement reached will remain unstable.
- Parties interact to establish the principle of just allocation "fair allocation" of water as the basis for their negotiations, and when they do not, further negotiations fail. This clarifies the importance of reaching a just and equitable water allocation scheme in order to move the negotiation to the collaborative region (see negotiation theory chapter 3)
- Justice as a package is a principle answer in complex water conflicts negotiations, in

preference to the over simplicity of dividing water resources.

- Water agreements are of a complex nature, Many agreements fail to sustain implementation notwithstanding their outcome.
- There are primarily two conditions of political viability of water-sharing (1) equity of the agreement or project (water allocation among states), and (2) control by each party of its own primary water sources. These two issues will have to be addressed early in negotiations. Clearly in the Jordan Israeli case these two were addressed but in a vague way, as there is no joint monitoring authority to control and check
- The success of Trans-boundary treaties is mostly judged by the manner in which the treaty itself was negotiated, this means the process speaks for the outcome and implementation
- Cheating is a short term strategy, building a long lasting relationships among riparian conflict parties requires honesty. Building trust is the most important ingredient for hydro-stability long lasting relationships.
- Holding secrecy and not opening

	the process of negotiation to the public will draw several question marks and create a cloud of suspicion around the whole process and prevent the public from engaging in the post treaty cooperation's
	• In order to attain a full cooperative trans-boundary agreement on the upper political level and the lower level it is important to include domestic discourse, such as the influence of interest groups, ideology and culture.
Water Diplomacy	• Joint problem-solving was established during the negotiation pre-treaty, they established a shred data knowledge and facilitated the reaching of a peace treaty.
	• Mutual Gains approach discusses the interest of both parties and moves beyond the position of each party, water was always on the lower political ladder during the bargaining negotiation, leaving many issues vague and unclear, this affected the mutual gains approach and weakened it
	• significant sensitivity, many other issues as the Jerusalem and Borders were more sensitive issues than water, but

nevertheless water was always played as a pressing card, and interlinked issue affecting the whole package of negotiation

- water professionals are deeply cognizant of the network's initial configurations
- Causes may not be proportional to effects,
- The more complex a proposal is technically.
- Politics highly affect water resources planning and management, in most cases water is used as a short-term strategy to enlarge the pie share on the account of the other party
- Move toward the best possible solution space. Implicit cooperation (among governments) has been successful even in advance of political solutions between the parties involved (Abukhater 2013; Susskind & Shafiqul Islam 2013) (e.g. Picnic Table talks, water-for-peace process). Nevertheless, explicit cooperation among independent organization has not preceded and was considered as naturalization with the enemy.

Table 19: Summary of the research second question.

The research focused on the characteristics of trans-boundary water conflict. Contrary to the "water war" paradigm that views water as the source of conflicts and wars, this research provided an alternative approach to conflict, showing that there is no evidence to support such thought, power imbalances plays a great role in trans-boundary water conflict. Negotiation on the other hand is most valuable feature of handling Trans-boundary water conflict,

5.4 Conclusions:

Jordan and Israel seemed aware of the unforeseen, yet impending consequences of reaching no settlement. The fact that the parties agreed to enter into negotiation and sign a water treaty is indicative of the amount of appreciable harm encountered by both parties in the absence of a water treaty, and suggests that the net benefits for the parties were considered to outweigh the costs of not signing a treaty. In that sense, the parties realized that they will encounter a certain degree of harm, whether water related or non-water related, if they relinquish the diplomatic option. In other words, the BATNA was identified as an undesirable course of action for all parties. This is because the appreciable harm for the parties is not confined to only loss of access to water resources, but also includes strategic harm in terms of impending conflict that is likely to occur in the absence of a treaty.

This Thesis contributes to the understanding of the characteristics of the trans-boundary water conflict between the Kingdom of Jordan and the state of Israel, and why parties chosen to reach an agreement over water, the future holds much more for both states if integrated into a full collaborative approach over water

Water agreements have to sides of outcomes, which are tangible and intangible products (Innes and Booher, 1999). Tangible products are easy to identify since they are the direct benefit from any negotiated agreements. These are concerned with the physical outcome of the negotiation, such as formal agreements, treaties, plans, and policies pertinent to the volumes of water allocated for each co-riparian, the time period, and the location of the withdrawal. It is also related to strategies put forth to maintain successful implementation processes. Intangible products, which in many cases are regarded as more important than the tangible products, are intellectual capital and non-water related matters, including mutual understanding of each other's interests and needs, shared definition of the problem and agreement on accurate data and quantitative models, and diplomatic and political capital (Innes and Booher, 1999). In evaluating and analyzing the aforementioned key treaties, value is placed on both tangible and intangible outcomes.

The research has showed that many characteristics shaped Trans-boundary water conflict, the research provide some insights for both researchers and practitioners, its showed that many theoretical assumptions lack true reality. The research also shaded light over the sensitivity of BATNA in trans-boundary water conflict, BATNA is considered a two way blade, and a careful assessment is required prior embarking on utilizing BATNA in water negotiation. In a nutshell, achieving Trans-boundary water equity is a major concern and employing a fair sharing process is essential in any water agreement.

Water diplomacy (Susskind & Shafiqul Islam 2013) (Abukhater 2013)provide a new way for analyzing water conflict, the way it works is by shifting states from positions toward their interest could provide a new opportunity toward managing and resolving trans-boundary water conflict.

Finally, the issues are not of disciplines and theory, but of people and water. I have shown that, just as nations have shaped the flow of water, so, too, did water shape the face of history. As Middle East peace negotiations attempt to lift the riparian's of the Jordan River watershed incrementally out of a perpetual cycle of violence, water can continue to ''lead'' the process towards ever-increasing cooperation. "It's Time to Peace".

References:

Abukhater, A., 2013. *Water as a Catalyst for Peace: Transboundary Water Management and Conflict Resolution*, Routledge.

Abukhater, A.B., 2010. *Equity in the Context of Bilateral, International Water Allocation Treaties in Arid Regions: An Interdisciplinary, Transformative Approach to Conflict Resolution*. The University of Texas at Austin.

Alkhaddar, R.M., Sheehy, W.J.S. & Al-Ansari, N., 2005. Jordan's Water Resources. *Water International*, 30(3), pp.294–303. Available at: http://www.tandfonline.com/doi/abs/10.1080/0250806 0508691870 [Accessed October 17, 2013].

Al-Kharabsheh, A. & Ta'any, R., 2005. Challenges of Water Demand Management in Jordan. *Water International*, 30(2), pp.210–219. Available at: http://www.tandfonline.com/doi/abs/10.1080/0250806 0508691861 [Accessed October 17, 2013].

Allan, J.A., 1998. Virtual water: A strategic resource. *Ground Water*, 36, pp.545–546.

Anon, 2013. The Syrian Influx. *Jordan Business*. Available at: http://www.jordan-business.net/cover_story/syrian-influx.

Attila, T., 2010. Reducing the Gap between International Water Law and Human Rights Law: The UNECE Protocol on Water and Health. *International Community Law Review*, 12, pp.267–285.

Baker, A., 2013. Will Syria's Refugee Crisis Drain Jordan of Its Water? Available at: http://world.time.com/2013/04/04/how-syrias-refugee-crisis-is-draining-jordans-scarce-water-supply/.

Bard, M.G., 2007. *Will Israel Survive*, Palgrave Macmillan.

Bartos, O.J. & Wehr, P., 2002. *USING CONFLICT THEORY*, Cambridge University Press.

Benvenisti, E., 2004. *Sharing Transboundary Resources*, London: Cambridge University Press.

Benvenisti, E. & Associa-, L., 2013. Collective Action in the Utilization of Shared Freshwater : The Challenges of International COLLECTIVE ACTION IN THE UTILIZATION OF SHARED FRESHWATER : THE CHALLENGES OF INTERNATIONAL WATER RESOURCES LAW codification. , 90(3), pp.384–415.

Berman, I. & Wihbey, P.M., 1999. The New Water Politics of the Middle East. *Strategic Review*. Available at: http://www.israeleconomy.org/strategic/water.htm.

Biswas, A.., 1994. *International waters of the middle east from euphrates-tigris to nile*, Oxford University Press.

Blair, D., 2013. Tens of thousands of Syrian refugees stranded on Jordanian border. Available at: http://www.telegraph.co.uk/news/worldnews/middleea

st/syria/10284503/Tens-of-thousands-of-Syrian-refugees-stranded-on-Jordanian-border.html.

Butler, M.J., 2009. *International Conflict Management* second edi., Routledge, London.

Crump, L., 2011. Negotiation Process and Negotiation Context. *International Negotiation*, 16, pp.197–227.

Dabelko, D., 2004. Water, Conflict, and Cooperation. *Water Management*, 10, pp.1–6. Available at: http://wilsoncenter.org/news/docs/Carius_Dabelko_W olf.pdf.

Dinar, A. & Lee, D.J., 1995. *Review of integrated approaches to river basin, planning, development and management*, Available at: http://www-wds.worldbank.org/servlet/WDSContentServer/WDSP /IB/1995/04/01/000009265_3970311121731/Rendered /PDF/multi_page.pdf.

Dolatyar, M., 2002. Water diplomacy in the Middle East. *University of Newcastle*. Available at: http://www.netcomuk.co.uk/~jpap/dolat.htm [Accessed April 27, 2014].

Doppler, W. et al., 2002. The impact of water price strategies on the allocation of irrigation water: the case of the Jordan Valley. *Agricultural Water Management*, 55(3), pp.171–182. Available at: http://linkinghub.elsevier.com/retrieve/pii/S03783774 01001937.

Drake, C., 2007. Water resource conflicts in the Middle East. *The Journal of geography*, 96(1), pp.4–12. Available at:

http://www.ncbi.nlm.nih.gov/pubmed/12178551 [Accessed December 7, 2013].

F, R. & Ury, W., 1991. *Getting to Yes: Negotiating Agreement Without Giving In* Revised 2n. Penguin Books, ed., New York, USA.

Faraj, M., 2014. Worst conditions for Jordan. Available at: http://www.farrajlawyer.com/viewTopic.php?topicId= 800 [Accessed January 2, 2014].

Faraj, M., 2014. Worst Conditions for Jordan. Available at: http://www.farrajlawyer.com/viewTopic.php?topicId= 800 [Accessed May 22, 2014].

Farooq Mitha, 2010. The Jordanian-Israeli Relationship: The Reality of "Cooperation." *Middle East Policy*, Vol. XVII(No. 2).

Fedorov, Y., 2013. the Syrian Cauldron. *Security Index: A Russian Journal on International Security*, 19(1), pp.83–88. Available at: http://www.tandfonline.com/doi/abs/10.1080/1993427 0.2013.759735 [Accessed October 18, 2013].

Fiadjoe, A., 2004. *ALTERNATIVE DISPUTE RESOLUTION: A DEVELOPING WORLD PERSPECTIVE*, Cavendish Publishing.

Fischhendler, I., 2008a. Ambiguity in Transboundary Environmental Dispute Resolution: The Israeli Jordanian Water Agreement. *Journal of Peace Research*, 45, pp.91–109.

Fischhendler, I., 2008b. Ambiguity in transboundary environmental dispute resolution: the Israel-Jordanian water agreement. *Journal of Peace Research*, (45), pp.91–110.

Fischhendler, I., 2008. When Ambiguity in Treaty Design Becomes Destructive: A Study of Transboundary Water. *Global Environmental Politics*, 8, pp.111–136.

Fisher, F.M., *Water and peace*, Available at: http://web.mit.edu/ffisher/www/waterpage/contentpag e/water.pdf.

Fisher, F.M., 2001. WATER: CASUS BELLI OR SOURCE OF COOPERATION. , pp.59–60.

Fisher, F.M. & Huber-Lee, A.T., 2011. The value of water: Optimizing models for sustainable management, infrastructure planning, and conflict resolution. *Desalination and Water Treatment*, 31(1-3), pp.1–23. Available at: http://www.tandfonline.com/doi/abs/10.5004/dwt.201 1.2401 [Accessed October 18, 2013].

Franklin M. Fisher, 2010. Water for Peace A Game Changer for israel, Paslestine and the Middle East.pdf. *WaterBiz*.

Franklin M. Fisher, 2002. Water Value, Water mamagement and Water Conflict.p. *GAIA*, (11).

Frederiksen, H.D., 1999. WATER : ISRAELIS TRATEGY , IMPLICATIONS PEACE AND THE VIABILITY OF PALESTINE. , pp.69–86.

Giordano, M. et al., 2013. The geography of water conflict and cooperation : internal pressures and international manifestations. , 168(4), pp.293–312.

Gleick, P.H., 2013. Water and conflict. *The MIT Press*, 18, pp.79–112.

Gleick, P.H., 1993. Water and Conflict: Fresh Water Resources and International Security. *International Security*, 18, pp.79–112.

Guan, D. & Hubacek, K., 2007. Assessment of regional trade and virtual water flows in China. *Ecological Economics*, 61, pp.159–170. Available at: <Go to ISI>://WOS:000245066400015\nhttp://www.sciencedi rect.com/science?_ob=MImg&_imagekey=B6VDY-4JDN6F9-5-3&_cdi=5995&_user=499905&_orig=search&_cover Date=02/15/2007&_sk=999389998&view=c&wchp=d GLbVlz-zSkWA&md5=40452fef2b436ac9417e472238972941 &ie=/sdarticle.pdf.

Guillermo J. Canoa, 1989. The Development of the Law of International Water Resources and the Work of the International Law Commission. *Water International*, (14), pp.167–171.

Gullickson, T. & Ramser, P., 1996. Negotiation in social conflict. *PsycCRITIQUES*, 41.

Haddadin, M. & Uri Shamir, 2003. *Jordan case study*, UNESCO-IHP. Paris: PCCP Series Publication.

Haddadin, M.J., 2002. *DIPLOMACY ON THE JORDAN: INTERNATIONAL CONFLICT AND NEGOTIATED RESOLUTION*, Springer.

Haftendorn, H., 2000. Water and international conflict. *Third World Quarterly*, 21, pp.51–68. Available at: <Go to ISI>://000084789700004.

Hajer, M. a., 1997. *The politics of environmental discourse: ecological modernization and the policy process*, Oxford: Clarendon Press.

Hanqin, X., 2003. *Transboundary Damage in International Law*, Cambridge University Press.

Harding, J.S. et al., 1999. Changes in agricultural intensity and river health along a river continuum. *Freshwater Biology*, 42(2), pp.345–357. Available at: http://doi.wiley.com/10.1046/j.1365-2427.1999.444470.x.

Hartmann, T., 2012. Wicked problems and clumsy solutions: Planning as expectation management. *Planning Theory*, 11(3), pp.242–256. Available at: http://plt.sagepub.com/cgi/doi/10.1177/147309521244 0427 [Accessed September 26, 2013].

Hazaimeh, H., 2014. Kingdom to trade desalinated water with Israel. *Jordan Times*. Available at: http://jordantimes.com/article/kingdom-to-trade-desalinated-water-with-israel.

Heather L. Beach, Jesse Hammer, J.J.H., 2000. *Transboundary freshwater dispute resolution*, The United Nations University.

Hussein, I.A.J., 2002. Water Planning in Jordan. *Water International*, 27(4), pp.468–475. Available at: http://www.tandfonline.com/doi/abs/10.1080/0250806 0208687034 [Accessed October 17, 2013].

Jain, S.K. & Singh, V.P., 2010. Water crisis. *Journal of Comparative Social Welfare*, 26(2-3), pp.215–237. Available at: http://www.tandfonline.com/doi/abs/10.1080/1748683 1003687618 [Accessed October 17, 2013].

Jerusalem Post July 16, 1996. water shortage. Available at: http://digilander.libero.it/asdfghj2/dossier/mf22.html# 16.

Kubursi, A., 2006. Water Scarcity and Water Wars in the Middle East? In *water global and local problem*. pp. 421–436.

Lankford, B. & Cour, J., 2005. From integrated to adaptive: a new framework for water resources management of river basins. In *Proceedings of the East Africa River Basin Management Conference. Morogoro, Tanzania, 7-9 March 2005*. Available at: http://www.iwmi.cgiar.org/Research_Impacts/Researc h_Themes/BasinWaterManagement/RIPARWIN/PDF s/finalised_LANKFORD_2_iwrm_conf_paper[1].pdf.

Lonergan, S.C., 2001. Water and Conflict: Rhetoric and Reality. In *Environmental Conflict*. pp. 109–124.

Lowi, M.R., 2003. *Water and Power*, Cambridge University Press.

Lukes, S., 1974. *Power: A radical view* 2nd editio., Macmillan: London.

Metz, T., 2002. Justice as Fairness: A Restatement. *Philosophical Review*, 111, pp.618–620.

Mirumachi, N. & Nakayama, M., 2007. Improving Methodologies for Transboundary Impact Assessment in Transboundary Watercourses: Navigation Channel Improvement Project of the Lancang-Mekong River from China-Myanmar Boundary Marker 243 to Ban Houei Sai of Laos. *International Journal of Water Resources Development*, 23(3), pp.411–425. Available at: http://www.tandfonline.com/doi/abs/10.1080/0790062 0701400153 [Accessed December 28, 2013].

Pahl-wostl, C. et al., 2007. Social Learning and Water Resources Management. *Ecology And Society*, 12, p.5. Available at: http://www.ibcperu.org/doc/isis/8547.pdf.

Pamukcu, K., 2003. WATER TRADE BETWEEN ISRAEL AND TURKEY: A START IN THE MIDDLE EAST. *MIDDLE EAST POLICY*, ,, VOL. X(NO. 4).

Platt, J., 1988. What can case studies do? *Studies in Qualitative Methodology*.

Priscoli, J.D., 1996. *CONFLICT RESOLUTION, COLLABORATION AND MANAGEMENT IN INTERNATIONAL AND REGIONAL WATER RESOURCES ISSUES,*

Priscoli, J.D. & Wolf, A.T., 2008. *Managing and Transforming Water Conflicts*, Cambridge University Press.

Rachael, G. et al., 2008. Negotiating over the allocation of water resources. In *Game Theory and Policymaking in Natural Resources and the Environment*. Routledge.

Raiffa, H., 1982. *The art and science of negotiation*, Available at: http://medcontent.metapress.com/index/A65RM03P4874243N.pdf\nhttp://books.google.com/books?hl=en&lr=&id=y-4T88h3ntAC&oi=fnd&pg=PA1&dq=The+art+and+science+of+negotiation&ots=4i5E0FZC0p&sig=s6UYFhMapmBibdWXQgMBQ7vXC2s.

Rawls, J., 2001. I. Justice as Fairness. *The Journal of Philosophy*, 54, p.653. Available at: http://www.jstor.org/stable/2021929?origin=crossref.

Roo, G. de & Silva, E.A., 2010. *A Planner's Encounter with Complexity*, ashgate.

Schelling, T.C., 1957. Bargaining, communication, and limited war. *Journal of Conflict Resolution*, 1, pp.19–36.

Scheumann, W. & Schiffler, M., 1998. *Water in the middle east*, Springer.

Schiffler, M., 1998. International Water Agreements: A Comparative View. In *Water in the Middle East*. pp. 31–44.

Selby, J., 2007. Beyond hydro-hegemony: gramsci, the national, and the trans-national. *Third International Workshop on Hydro-Hegemony, London School of Economic*.

Selby, J., 2005. The Geopolitics of Water in the Middle East: fantasies and realities. *Third World Quarterly*, 26(2), pp.329–349. Available at:

http://www.tandfonline.com/doi/abs/10.1080/0143659
042000339146 [Accessed October 18, 2013].

Sherman, M., 1999. *The Politics of Water in the Middle East*, Macmillan Press.

Sherman, M., 1993. Water as an Impossible Impasse in the Israel-Arab Conflict. *Nativ Center for Policy Research*.

Shuval, H., 2011. Comments on "Confronting water in the Israeli–Palestinian peace agreement" by David Brooks and Julie Trottier [Journal of Hydrology 382/1–4, pp. 103–114]. *Journal of Hydrology*, 397, pp.146–148.

Shuval, H. & Dweik, H., 2007. *Water Resources in the Middle East*, Springer.

Sivakumar, B., 2011. Water crisis: From conflict to cooperation—an overview. *Hydrological Sciences Journal*, 56(4), pp.531–552. Available at: http://www.tandfonline.com/doi/abs/10.1080/0262666 7.2011.580747 [Accessed October 17, 2013].

Steenhuis, G.H.-W. and T., 2010. Losing Paradise by Gail Holst-Warhaft and Tammo Steenhuis. *Ashgate*, p.234. Available at: http://www.ashgate.com/isbn/9780754675730.

Susskind, L. & Shafiq Islam, 2013. *Water Diplomacy: A Negotiated Approach to Managing Complex Water Networks*, Routledge.

Susskind, L.E., 1994. *Environmental Diplomacy*, OXFORD UNIVERSITY PRESS.

Susskind, L.E. & Shafiqul Islam, 2013. *Water Diplomacy: A Negotiated Approach to Managing Complex Water Networks*, Routledge.

Swyngedouw, E., 2005. Dispossessing H2O: the contested terrain of water privatization. *Capitalism Nature Socialism*, 16(1), pp.81–98.

Swyngedouw, E., 2008. Geopolitics of Water – The Power of Water. *Globalgeopolitics Weblog*.

TALOZI, S.A., 2007. *Integrated water resource management and security in middle east* A. A. Clive Lipchin, Eric Pallant, Danielle Saranga, ed., Springer.

Trolldalen, J.M., 1997. Troubled waters in the Middle East : the process towards the first Regional Water Declaration between Jordan , Palestinian Authority , and Israel. , 21(97), pp.101–108.

Trottier, J. & Slack, P. eds., 2004. *Managing Water Resources, Past and Present,*

UNRWA, 2013. Jordan, Facts & figures. Available at: http://www.unrwa.org/where-we-work/jordan.

Velma I. Grover, 2007. *Water a source of conflict and cooperation*, Science Publishers.

Wardam, B., 2004. More politics then water: Water rights in Jordan. *Global Issues Paper*, (11), pp.60–107. Available at: http://www.boell.de/sites/default/files/assets/boell.de/images/download_de/internationalepolitik/GIP11_Jordan_Batir_Wardam.pdf.

Westing, A.H., 1986. *Global resources and international conflict: environmental factors in strategic policy and action*, Oxford University Press.

Williams, P., 2002. Nile co-operation through hydro-realpolitik ? *Third World Quarterly*, 23(6), pp.1189–1196. Available at: http://www.tandfonline.com/doi/abs/10.1080/0143659022000036577 [Accessed January 2, 2014].

Wolf, A.T., 1995. *Hydropolitics along the Jordan River: Scarce water and its impact on the Arab–Israeli conflict*, United Nations University Press.

Wolf, A.T., 1996. Middle East Water Conflicts and Directions for Conflict Resolution. , (March).

Wolf, A.T., Yoffe, S.B. & Giordano, M., 2003. International waters : identifying basins at risk. , 5, pp.29–60.

Woltjer, J., 2004. Consensus Planning. In *Enviromental and infrastrcuture planning*. Groningen: GEO Press.

World Bank, 1996. From Scarcity to Security: Averting a Water Crisis in the Middle East and North Africa.

Yoffe, S., Wolf, A.T. & Giordano, M., 2003. Conflict and Cooperation Over International Freshwater Resources: Indicators of Basins at Risk. *Journal of the American Water Resources Association*, 39, pp.1109–1126. Available at: http://onlinelibrary.wiley.com.proxy.library.oregonstate.edu/doi/10.1111/j.1752-1688.2003.tb03696.x/abstract.

Zartman, 2001. Negotiating Internal Conflict: Incentives and Intractability. *International Negotiation*, 6, pp.297–302.

Zartman, I.W., 2001. Preventing Deadly Conflict. *Security Dialogue*, 32, pp.137–154.

Zartman, I.W. & Rubin, J.Z., 2002. *Power and Negotiation,*

Zartman, W., 1975. Negotiations: Theory and Reality. *Journal of International Affairs*, 29, p.69.

Zeitoun, M., 2008. *Power and water in the middle east*, I.B.Tauris & Co Ltd.

Zeitoun, M. & Allan, J.A., 2008. Applying hegemony and power theory to transboundary water analysis. *Water Policy*, 10 Supplem, pp.3–12.

Zeitoun, M. & Elisa, A., 2010. *Transboundary Water Management: Principles and Practice* A. Earle, ed., Earthscan Publications Ltd.

Zeitoun, M. & Warner, J., 2006a. Hydro-hegemony – a framework for analysis of trans-boundary water conflicts. *Water Policy*, 8(5), p.435. Available at: http://www.iwaponline.com/wp/00805/wp008050435. htm [Accessed December 18, 2013].

Zeitoun, M. & Warner, J., 2006b. Hydro-hegemony – a framework for analysis of trans-boundary water conflicts. *Water Policy*, 8, p.435.

جامعة النجاح الوطنية *إلحياة مفاوضات* .عريقات, ص., 2008

Appendix A

Interview Questions:

Process questions:
Q1: Can you walk me through the process of negotiation and conflict resolution efforts
Q2: How do you characterize the negotiation style: zero-sum, interest-based or position-based?
Q3: Did any of the parties suggest incorporating conflict resolution techniques, such joint fact finding (JFF), use of mediators, arbitration, modern and indigenous or other conflict resolution techniques?
Q5: Did the parties mutually agree on a third party involvement/facilitation/mediation?
Q6: Was the negotiation process incremental or did it occur all in one event?
Q7: What, if any, was the role of the public in the making of the treaty?

Planning Analysis questions:
Q1: Prior to the negotiation process, was there any data mediation efforts and JFF to ensure that everyone agreed on factual information?
Q2: Did the makers of the treaty consider the population growth rate, annual water budget, *per capita* consumption rate, consumption by sector, or use a water demand model?
Q3: How do you characterize the allocation scheme: needs-based or rights-based?

Structure of the agreement questions:
Q1: How well did the makers of the treaty consider quantity or quality?

Q2: How was water allocated: time-based allocation or volumetric-based only or both?

Q3: Did the makers of the treaty consider the resultant benefits from water use directly or merely volumetric water allocation *per se*?

Q4: How did the treaty incorporate prioritization of different uses and users?

Q5: Would you say that the agreement is flexible to new events and circumstances such as adaptability to drought and extreme hydro-events?

Q6: Did the treaty consider both environmental and non-environmental factors? How did you decide on which to keep in the treaty and those outside?

Q7: How did the treaty ensure the compliance mechanism and monitoring of its implementation? What, if any, problems have occurred with compliance? Why do you think these problems occurred?

Overall questions:
Q1: If you were to do this differently, what would you do?

Q2: What was the most interesting/frustrating experience you had during negotiation?
Did you ever at any point of the negotiation think of quitting (psychological break downs)? When and why?

Q3: What do you like/dislike the most about the process and outcome of this agrement? What works and does not work?

Q4: Please give me your opinion on how fair/equitable you think the agreement was for both sides? On a scale of 1-5 (5 being highest) please rank the degree to which the agreement is fair/equitable?

Q5: Explain why you think so?

Q6: What could've been done differently to improve the agreement, given your experience to date?

Q7: In your opinion, what are the most important elements that could be incorporated in binational water negotiations to move from non-cooperation to cooperation and balance the agreement?

Q8: Can you think of a better water treaty in terms of equity of outcomes?

Appendix B

Water Agreement

Annex II

http://www.kinghussein.gov.jo/peacetreaty.html

Water Related Matters

Pursuant to Article 6 of the Treaty, Jordan and Israel agreed on the following Articles on water related matters:

Article I: **Allocation**

Water from the Yarmouk River

A. Summer period - 15th May to 15th October of each year. Israel pumps (12) MCM and Jordan gets the rest of the flow.

B. Winter period - 16th October to 14th May of each year. Israel pumps (13) MCM and Jordan is entitled to the rest of the flow subject to provisions outlined herein below: Jordan concedes to Israel pumping an additional (20) MCM from the Yarmouk in winter in return for Israel conceding to transferring to Jordan during the summer period the quantity specified in paragraph (2.a) below from the Jordan River.

C. In order that waste of water will be minimized, Jordan and Israel may use, downstream of Adassiya Diversion/point 121, excess flood water that is not usable and will evidently go to waste unused.

Water from the Jordan River

A. Summer period - 15th May to 15th October of each year. In return for the additional water that Jordan concedes to Israel in winter in accordance with paragraph (1.b) above, Israel concedes to transfer to Jordan in the summer period (20) MCM from the Jordan River directly upstream form Deganya gates on the river. Jordan shall pay the operation and maintenance cost of such transfer through existing systems (not including capital cost) and shall bear the total cost of any new transmission system. A separate protocol shall regulate this transfer.

B. Winter period - 16th October to 14th May of each year. Jordan is entitled to store for its use a minimum average of (20) MCM of the floods in the Jordan River south of its confluence with the Yarmouk (as outlined in Article II below). Excess floods that are not usable and that will otherwise be wasted can be utilized for the benefit of the two Parties including pumped storage off the course of the river.

C. In addition to the above, Israel is entitled to maintain its current uses of the Jordan River waters between its confluence with the Yarmouk and its confluence with Wadi Yabis/Tirat Zvi. Jordan is entitled to an annual quantity equivalent to that of Israel, provided however, that Jordan's use will not harm the quantity or quality of the above Israeli uses. The Joint Water Committee (outlined in Article VI below) will survey existing uses for documentation and prevention of appreciable harm.

D. Jordan is entitled to an annual quantity of (10) MCM of desalinated water from the desalination of about (20) MCM of saline springs now diverted to the Jordan River. Israel will explore the possibility of financing the operation and maintenance cost of the supply to Jordan of this desalinated water (not including capital cost). Until the desalination facilities are operational, and upon the entry into force of the Treaty, Israel will supply Jordan (10) MCM of Jordan River water from the same location as in (2.a) above, outside the summer period and during dates Jordan selects, subject to the maximum capacity of transmission.

Additional Water

Jordan and Israel shall cooperate in finding sources for the supply to Jordan of an additional quantity of (50) MCM/year of water of drinkable standards. To this end, the Joint Water Committee will develop, within one year from the entry into force of the Treaty, a plan for the supply to Jordan of the above mentioned additional water. This plan will be forwarded to the respective governments for discussion and decision.

Operation and Maintenance

A. Operation and maintenance of the systems on Israeli territory that supply Jordan with water, and their electricity supply, shall be Israel's responsibility. The operation and maintenance of the new systems that serve only Jordan will be contracted at Jordan's expense to authorities or companies selected by Jordan.

B. Israel will guarantee easy unhindered access of personnel and equipment to such new systems for operation and maintenance. This subject will be further detailed in the agreements to be signed between Israel and the authorities or companies selected by Jordan.

Article II: Storage

1. Jordan and Israel shall cooperate to build a diversion/storage dam on the Yarmouk River directly downstream of the Adassiya Diversion/point 121.

2. The purpose is to improve the diversion efficiency into the King Abdullah Canal of the water allocation of the Hashemite Kingdom of Jordan, and possibly for the diversion of Israel's allocation of the river water. Other purposes can be mutually agreed.

3. Jordan and Israel shall cooperate to build a system of water storage on the Jordan River, along their common boundary, between its confluence with the Yarmouk River and its confluence with Wadi Yabis/Tirat Zvi, in order to implement the provision of paragraph (2.b) of Article I above. The storage system can also be made to

4. Accommodate more floods; Israel may use up to (3) MCM/year of added storage capacity.

5. Other storage reservoirs can be discussed and agreed upon mutually.

Article III: Water Quality and Protection

1. Jordan and Israel each undertake to protect, within their own jurisdiction, the shared waters of the Jordan and Yarmouk Rivers, and Araba/Arava groundwater, against any pollution, contamination, harm or unauthorized withdrawals of each other's allocations.

2. For this purpose, Jordan and Israel will jointly monitor the quality of water along their boundary, by use of jointly established monitoring stations to be operated under the guidance of the Joint Water Committee.

3. Jordan and Israel will each prohibit the disposal of municipal and industrial wastewater into the courses of the Yarmouk and the Jordan Rivers before they are treated to standards allowing their unrestricted agricultural use.

4. Implementation of this prohibition shall be completed within three years from the entry into force of the Treaty.

5. The quality of water supplied from one country to the other at any given location shall be equivalent to the quality of the water used from the same location by the supplying country.

6. Saline springs currently diverted to the Jordan River are earmarked for desalination within four years. Both countries shall cooperate to ensure that the resulting brine will not be disposed of in the Jordan River or in any of its tributaries. Jordan and Israel will protect water systems each in its own territory, supplying water to the other, against any pollution, contamination, harm or unauthorized withdrawal of each other's allocations.

Article IV: **Groundwater in Wadi Araba/Emek Ha'arava**

1. In accordance with the provisions of this Treaty, some wells drilled and used by Israel along with their associated systems fall on the Jordanian side of the borders. These wells and systems are under Jordan's sovereignty. Israel shall retain the use of these wells and systems in the quantity and quality detailed in an Appendix to this Annex, that shall be jointly prepared by 31st December, 1994. Neither country shall take, nor cause to be taken, any measure that may appreciably reduce the yields or quality of these wells and systems.

2. Throughout the period of Israel's use of these wells and systems, replacement of any well that may fail among them shall be licensed by Jordan in accordance with the laws and regulations then in effect. For this purpose, the failed well shall be treated as though it was drilled under license from the competent Jordanian authority at the time of its drilling. Israel shall supply Jordan with the log of each of the wells and the technical information about it to be kept on record. The replacement well shall be connected to the Israeli electricity and water systems.

3. Israel may increase the abstraction rate from wells and systems in Jordan by up to (10) MCM/year above the yields referred to in paragraph 1 above, subject to a determination by the Joint Water Committee that this undertaking is hydrogeologically feasible and does not harm existing Jordanian uses. Such increase is to be carried out within five years from the entry into force of the Treaty.

4. Operation and Maintenance

    A. Operation and maintenance of the wells and systems on Jordanian territory that supply Israel with water, and their electricity supply shall be Jordan's responsibility. The operation and maintenance of these wells and systems will be contracted at Israel's expense to authorities or companies selected by Israel.

    B. Jordan will guarantee easy unhindered access of personnel and equipment to such wells and systems for operation and maintenance. This subject will be further detailed in the agreements to be signed between Jordan and the authorities or companies selected by Israel.

Article V: Notification and Agreement

1. Artificial changes in or of the course of the Jordan and Yarmouk Rivers can only be made by mutual agreement.

2. Each country undertakes to notify the other, six months ahead of time, of any intended projects which are likely to change the flow of either of the above rivers along their common boundary, or the quality of such flow. The subject will be discussed in the

Joint Water Committee with the aim of preventing harm and mitigating adverse impacts such projects may cause.

Article VI: **Co-operation**

1. Jordan and Israel undertake to exchange relevant data on water resources through the Joint Water Committee.

2. Jordan and Israel shall co-operate in developing plans for purposes of increasing water supplies and improving water use efficiency, within the context of bilateral, regional or international cooperation.

Article VII: **Joint Water Committee**

1. For the purpose of the implementation of this Annex, the Parties will establish a Joint Water Committee comprised of three members from each country.

2. Governments specify its work procedures, the frequency of its meetings, and the details of its scope of work. The Committee may invite experts and/or advisors as may be required.

3. The Committee may form, as it deems necessary, a number of specialized sub- committees and assign them technical tasks. In this context, it is agreed that these sub-committees will include a northern sub-committee and a southern sub-committee, for the management on the ground of the mutual water resources in these sectors.

Source: http://www.kinghussein.gov.jo/peacetreaty.html